THE TAO OF JUNG

THE
TAO
OF
JUNG

The Way of Integrity

DAVID ROSEN, M.D.

VIKING ARKANA

VIKING ARKANA
Published by the Penguin Group
Penguin Books USA Inc., 375 Hudson Street, New York, New York 10014, U.S.A.
Penguin Books Ltd, 27 Wrights Lane, London W8 5TZ, England
Penguin Books Australia Ltd, Ringwood, Victoria, Australia
Penguin Books Canada Ltd, 10 Alcorn Avenue, Toronto, Ontario, Canada M4V 3B2
Penguin Books (N.Z.) Ltd, 182–190 Wairau Road, Auckland 10, New Zealand

Penguin Books Ltd, Registered Offices: Harmondsworth, Middlesex, England

First published in 1996 by Viking Penguin, a division of Penguin Books USA Inc.

1 3 5 7 9 10 8 6 4 2

Page 198 constitutes an extension of this copyright page.

LIBRARY OF CONGRESS CATALOGING-IN-PUBLICATION DATA
Rosen, David H., 1945–
The Tao of Jung: the way of integrity/David Rosen.
p. cm.
Includes bibliographical references and index.
ISBN 0 670 86069 7 (alk. paper)
1. Psychoanalysis and religion. 2. Taoism—Psychology. 3. Jungian psychology.
4. Jung, C. G. (Carl Gustav), 1875–1961. I. Title.
BF175.4.R44R66 1996
150.19′54′092—dc20 96–10240

This book is printed on acid-free paper.

Printed in the United States of America
Set in Bembo
DESIGNED BY BRIAN MULLIGAN

For Sarah
and her Tao

East and West
Can no longer be kept apart.

GOETHE

Contents

Part II Post-Freud

Illustrations

Acknowledgments

For generous assistance and kind friendship while in Zürich, I sincerely thank Franz Jung, Peter Jung, and Karil Rauss. For sustaining encouragement and support, I'm indebted to Marie Louise von Franz and the late C. A. Meier. A sincere thank you to Professor Mingshen Zhou, Hallie Duke, and Michael McCloud for early research and meaningful discussions. I am beholden and grateful to the estate of C. G. Jung for permission to reproduce eleven pictures, paintings, and photos of and by C. G. Jung. A particular acknowledgment is made to Hing Wah Hatch, a Chinese-American artist, who did the extraordinary calligraphy. I express deep gratitude to the following readers and critics, who helped to make this a better book: Kathi Appelt, Deborah Brock, Mary Lenn Dixon, Maria-Cristina Garcia, Holly Huston, Carol Lawson, Robert Newman, Ellen Russon, Arnold Vedlitz, and Joel Weishaus. A special acknowledgment and thank you is extended to Jacinta Frawley, my typist in Zürich and my initial reader and critic. As a Jungian analyst in training, Jacinta also brought to bear knowledge of analytical psychology as well as keen questions regarding misunderstandings and areas that needed clarification. I will forever be grateful to Jacinta, her good husband, Oliver, and little Timothy, who was born during the writing of the initial manuscript. I also want to express my extreme gratitude to Amy Hunnicutt, my Texas typist, who was always cheerful and competent throughout the preparation of the final manuscript. In addition, heartfelt thanks are due my literary agent, Ned Leavitt, and my editor and assistant editor at Viking Penguin, David Stanford and Kristine Puopolo, respectively.

The Tao

The Tao

The Tao (the Way) is both fixed and moving at
the same time. The Tao governs the individual
just as it does visible and invisible nature (earth
and heaven). On the left side of the ancient
Chinese pictograph, which is linked to the
earth, the upper part signifies going step-by-
step, but the line underneath connotes standing
still. On the right side is a head with hair
above, which is associated with heaven, and interpreted as the beginning or source. The original meaning of the whole pictograph is of the
Way, which, though fixed itself, leads from beginning to end and back to the beginning.

Preface

Life can only be understood backwards: but it must be lived forwards.

SÖREN KIERKEGAARD

I was drawn to Taoism long ago, when I first read Lao Tzu. I felt he was writing to me. It was the same experience I had when I first read Carl Jung. Gradually, I noticed that Jung himself, from a very early age, was Taoist in his approach to life. This book was conceived when I brought these two important interests of mine together and realized that they were like streams flowing into the same river.

The Tao of Jung is about Jung's way, but it also reflects my way. An undertaking such as this is bound to be personal. After I arrived in Zürich, where I wrote this book, I came across a passage in a letter of Jung's that spoke to me:

. . . be simple and always take the next step. You needn't see it in advance, but you can look back at it afterwards. There is no "how" of life, one just does it. . . . It seems, however, to be terribly difficult for you *not* to be complicated and to do what is simple and closest to hand. . . . So climb down from the mountain of your humility and follow your nose. That is *your* way.[1]

On the eve of my trip to Switzerland, I had had an inspiring dream: I was in a place that looked and felt like the Swiss Alps. I was with a woman, not anyone I knew, but she seemed like a friend. Far below was a mountain village with a river running through it. There was a chute going straight down to the village, but I did not take this shortcut. Rather I walked slowly and descended with the woman.

In the dream, the woman represents my creative muse, *anima*, or soul. The dream is related to the Tao in that it signaled me to move forward and proceed slowly and naturally down the mountain path together with my feminine side.

Jung posited that dreams are messages to us from the ultimate creative source: the Self (or Tao). My dream, therefore, affirmed my decision to go alone to Zürich to write *The Tao of Jung*. Originally, I had wanted my wife to accompany me on the trip, but she chose not to do so. This was understandable, since she had her own profession to attend to. However, my decision and my firmness and resolution to go precipitated a crisis. My wife did not want me to go. She portrayed it as being irresponsible. I felt torn, especially because my three daughters were caught in the middle of such a struggle. I also thought that it would be a passing storm like many we had weathered before. I thought that it would all work out and that the absence would make the heart grow fonder. I knew that a colleague had been to Australia recently, alone, on a sabbatical for the same time period. His wife chose to stay and work at her profession, and their marriage survived and all seemed well. It came down to this: a deep, mysterious force was guiding me to cross the Atlantic, do the research, and write the book. I've now come to appreciate that research is really me-search. Little did I know when I set out on this journey that I was to experience the most significant death and rebirth experience of my life. The Tao had spoken: my journey of "creative quietude" was to be endured alone.

I moved into my new abode near Zürich. It was an electrician's ground-floor apartment in the small village of Bassersdorf. I was astonished when I learned that this place was available because the tenant was taking an extended trip to the East. Half of his living room was Oriental and the other half Swiss. I told this fellow that I would be writing a book about Jung and Taoism and also journeying to the East—in a manner of speaking—while all the time remaining in his apartment. During my first week to ten days in Switzerland, the strangest thing happened. Now I realize that it was prophetic of what was to come. I felt as if I was dying. I thought it was my heart, which ached, and at times the pain was unbearable—especially the pain that radiated down my left arm. Through a friend, I got to a Swiss internist, who examined me and took an electrocardiogram. Everything was normal. The doctor thought it was pain from an old left-sided cervical disk injury. I was reassured that I was not physically dying, but it turned out that I was psychically going through a death experience. At the time, I didn't realize fully how the personal experience of my own crisis would sensitize me to my research and the unfolding crises of Jung's life.

Once I recovered, I visited Marie Louise von Franz and C. A. Meier, two esteemed Jungian analysts and long-term colleagues of Jung's. In a way, one could say that they know Jung and his psychology better than most living Jungians. I asked each of them if they thought Jung was Taoist. Marie Louise von Franz said, "Yes, Jung favored Taoism, and he lived the Taoist philosophy." C. A. Meier agreed: "Yes, he was Taoist, and today people don't realize that his psychology of opposites is virtually the same as Taoism.

People want to make him into something he was not. He was tied to Nature and its contradictions. Yet, he was devoutly spiritual and clearly more Taoist than anything else." Their comments confirmed for me that I was on the right path.

When I first set out to explore Jung's world (his life and psychology) and how it related to Taoism, I did not fully appreciate how closely both reflected my own nature. It came home solidly when I visited Bollingen, which had been an aspiration of mine for thirty years, ever since I had read *Memories, Dreams, Reflections* when I was nineteen. There I could see and feel how Jung had made peace with his psyche and Nature. At Bollingen, I tasted the bliss of solitude. I sensed what tranquillity reigned over this ground, isolated from all things of the world. Bollingen, made of stone, with its many carvings and sculptures, served a transcendent function for Jung. In the original Tower building, he painted a huge mandala above his bed that is of the East, Tibetan-like, and Taoist. White light comes to a center point out of multiple spheres, twelve in the first circular group and twenty-four in the second. Everything radiates out of an azure blue sealike background. The outer four boundaries are red and appear to be flames. This mandala represents the Taoist concept of light (the secret of the golden flower) emanating from the union of water (*yin*/feminine) and fire (*yang*/masculine).

Aniela Jaffé, who knew Jung better than most, maintained that he was in his element at Bollingen.

> Here his feeling for Nature showed itself in a way it couldn't do in Küsnacht. . . . it was a genuine rootedness in his own earth, a communion with the whole countryside. . . . But one thing gave Bollingen its special quality: silence. Jung was a great one for silence. . . . It was a vital necessity for him to sink himself in a profound introversion; this was the fountainhead of helpful and vivifying powers. Creative ideas took shape in the inner and outer stillness.[2]

Writing this book has changed me. I am now quieter and more attuned to the natural world. In place of radio and television, which I went without for seven months, I got to know the brook in Bassersdorf. I walked on Wanderwegs. I befriended birds, woods, and stones and I wrote haiku poems as a form of meditation on nature and creativity.

My hope is that this book, besides informing readers of Taoism and Jung's psychology, inspires and leads them toward an integration of the principles and energies of yin (the receptive and feminine) and yang (the active and masculine), facilitating a more harmonious and peaceful way of life. As we all know, this is desperately needed in our increasingly hectic and stressful world. Jung's psychology, like Taoism, involves having the ego and one's personal being in a secondary position to the Self or Tao, which is the Supreme Being, Primary Essence, or Eternal Way.

It wasn't until I fully embarked upon the journey of writing this book that I realized it had to be taken alone. The word "alone" derives from "all one." How else would I come to know that I am one with nature, the river, and the Tao without experiencing it? So in Switzerland I took the long way down with my muse.

Being apart from my family for over half a year was a major sacrifice by all concerned, but sacrifice in its deepest sense means to "make sacred." The project proved to be a turning point. The key was (and is) to take the middle path (as did Lao Tzu and Jung) through the dark valley between the mountain peaks of danger and opportunity and to emerge more whole into the light. Herein lies the mystery and meaning of the Tao: to make the sacrifice and surrender to the Eternal Way of integrity.

—David Rosen
Bassersdorf,
Switzerland

THE TAO OF JUNG

Introduction

All movements are accomplished in six stages, and the seventh brings
return. . . . Seven is the number of young light, and it arises when six,
the number of the great darkness, is increased by one.

THE I CHING [1]

Carl Jung's life and his psychology reveal the Tao at work. His
description of the natural world of the psyche is similar to the
natural world as described by Taoists. The essence of both
philosophies is the integration of opposites, that Taoist principle
of yin/yang, which leads to wholeness.

Jung, the Westerner, lived in the introverted spirit of many
Eastern traditions, while not giving up the extraverted world into
which he was born. He sought to bridge the masculine paragon of
the West and the feminine ideal of the East.[2]

Danger

Jung started out as a Freudian; leaving Freud turned out to be the major crisis in his life. The Chinese represent crisis with two pictographs: danger and opportunity. The Tao enabled Jung to walk through the convoluted valley of danger (death) and opportunity (rebirth) and end up as a more complete person.

The Tao of Jung is organized in two parts, each a triad of three chapters. Part I covers the first three phases of Jung's life (birth to the break with Freud) and is based on the ancient Chinese pictograph of *danger*.

Part II focuses on the last three segments of Jung's life (resolution of his mid-life crisis to his death) and is based on the pictograph of *opportunity*.

This book is arranged in six chapters, each of which is organized around a crisis specific to a developmental stage of Jung's life. In each chapter, the resolution of the crisis is linked to the

Opportunity

emergence of concepts of Jung's psychology and Taoist principles. The purpose of this introduction, as the seventh part, is to begin to shine light on what many have called the dark, mysterious, and mystical life of Carl Jung. As will be seen, the truth is that by the time Jung died, his life was luminous, balanced, and in harmony with the *Tao*.

Jung's life, divided into six parts, represents a Chinese hexagram. The upper trigram, *danger* (see the pictograph for part I), pertains to the first three chapters, which I will review briefly here.

The first chapter, "Sunrise to the Eve of Pubescence: Becoming a Separate Individual," covers unconscious Taoist forces at work from Jung's birth in 1875 through his early school years. Even at this time, we see Jung as a distinct person. This beginning stage is represented by the initial part of the first pictograph of danger, "the individual" ⁊. The danger for Jung, as for any young person, is that he will not become his *true self*. Fortunately, I am able to trace the way Jung begins to self-actualize. Jung's process allows me to compare the concept of the Self in his psychology with the Tao,[3] and then to show how the ego (one's identity) or "center of consciousness" emerges from both.

Chapter 2, "Puberty to Psychiatry: Resolution of Jung's Early-Life Crisis," discusses Jung's adolescent years, university study, completion of medical school (1900), and his choice of psychiatry as a specialty. The image of "the cliff" Γ, the second aspect of the *danger* pictograph, is an apt representation of the "early-life crisis" of adolescence and young adulthood. It is during these critical years that Jung's father died, setting the stage for a father complex (that is, a conflict or problem with one's father), and the need to work it through with an older man. Regarding Jung's psychological concepts, this section focuses on persona roles, shadow, and complex formation. The Taoist principles discussed are similar: those of persona (mask) and shadow.

Chapter 3 describes "The Freud Years: Emergence of Jung's Mid-Life Crisis." Jung first read Freud's *Interpretation of Dreams* in 1900, but he did not fully understand Freud's *magnum opus* until 1903. Jung started corresponding with Freud in 1906, when he sent him his book *Diagnostic Association Studies*. Both Jung and Freud believed in the revolutionary concept that psychiatric symptoms and disorders were understandable and therefore meaningful. Jung met Freud in 1907, when he was thirty-two and Freud was fifty-one. By 1908, Jung had become an ardent follower of Freud, who was old enough to be his father. Freud considered Jung to be the "Crown Prince" of psychoanalysis and his personal successor. However, after several disputes involving issues of integrity and differences in their theoretical approaches, Jung broke with Freud in 1913. Jung's seminal work *Psychology of the Unconscious* (1912, later retitled *Symbols of Transformation*) precipitated the break. Also in 1913, Jung resigned his professorship at the University of Zürich. The third part of the *danger* picto-

graph is an image of a measured response ㄹ. It is characterized by slow and cautious movement, which enables one to preserve one's dignity. This was a time when Jung began to confront his negative father complex and the trickster aspect of his personality. Jung resolved a suicidal crisis in December of 1913 by instead committing "egocide" (symbolic death) and choosing new life, rather than self-destruction. In other words, a negative ego-image and identity connected with Freud had to be killed. It is noteworthy that prior to their falling out, Freud expressed the concern that Jung wanted to kill him. However, what really needed to be killed was Jung's *false self*, that is, his ego identity as a Freudian. The Taoist and Jungian principle of nonviolence to self and others is discussed.

The lower trigram, *opportunity* (see the pictograph for Part II), refers to the last three chapters.

Chapter 4 concerns "Creative Illness: Resolution of Jung's Mid-Life Crisis." After the 1913 break with Freud, Jung, at the age of thirty-eight, became profoundly depressed and lost in the dark abyss of the collective unconscious. Jung had a vision of Elijah (who later evolved into the positive spiritual figure of Philemon and then into an evil demon named Ka) and a blind Salome. Jung was clearly blind to his feminine side, as manifested in the affairs he had with two patients, Sabina Spielrein and Toni Wolff. Yet, following a symbolic death experience of his former ego or *false self*, Jung underwent a rebirth of his *true self*. In 1916, as if to memorialize this experience, Jung wrote the mysterious and Taoist-like "Seven Sermons to the Dead." He then carried out significant work outlining his psychology: *Two Essays on Analytical Psychology* (1917) and *Psychological Types* (1921). *Psychological Types* contains numerous references to Taoism; it is here that Jung first formally introduces the central Taoist concept that the union of opposites leads to harmony, a concept that became the primary maxim of Jung's own psychology. In 1922, at the age of forty-seven, he purchased the Bollingen property and, meaningfully, after the death of his mother in 1923, he began building the first Tower at Bollingen. As represented by the first element of the *opportunity* pictograph ✗, which is like a tree, Jung put down roots and branched out. Building his Bollingen Tower was an active imagination task of immense proportion, which helped him work through his negative mother complex. When Jung broke from Freud, he went through a major sacrifice (ego-death), which created needed sacred space within. At this point in his life, the wise old man archetype was clearly activated in Jung. The parallel Taoist principle of letting go of ego and emptying out the psyche so spirit and soul can enter is discussed.

Chapter 5, "Union of East and West: Emergence of Jung's Late-Life Crisis," represents more of Jung's serious effort to unify his psyche. Through his anima (the feminine aspect of his psyche), Jung glimpsed the Self, which facilitated transcendence of the opposites and further integration of his personality. This is when we see movement toward the union of Eastern and Western views. In the next portion of the second pictograph, 𝟖𝟖 two sets of two cocoons are being held in pairs by a light thread that is symbolic of union and incubation. Out of the cocoons, butterflies will emerge, which symbolize the feminine, the soul, and transformation. Jung's psychological concept of anima, or soul, equals the Taoist principle of yin, the dark and feminine. The similarity of anima and yin, as well as other concepts like the Self and the Tao, catalyzed Jung's interest in Chinese philosophy and spirituality. When Jung was fifty-two years old, he began a collaboration with Richard Wilhelm on an ancient Chinese Taoist text, *The Secret of the Golden Flower* (1929).

Despite Jung's profound professional and personal work during the Nazi period, he made a tragic detour off the Taoist path. Psychological blindness and deafness left him gripped by an unconscious power complex and formidable shadow problem that led to some significant mistakes. In 1935, at the age of sixty, Jung wrote a psychological commentary on *The Tibetan Book of the Great Lib-*

eration, signaling a return to his Eastern path. Four years later, when he was fully conscious of the horrors of Nazism—he himself was blacklisted and his books burned—he wrote both a psychological commentary on *The Tibetan Book of the Dead* (1939) and a foreword to D. T. Suzuki's *Introduction to Zen Buddhism* (1939). After a fall in 1944, at the age of sixty-nine, Jung suffered a heart (and soul) attack, leading to a near-death experience, which allowed for the possibility of true healing based on forgiveness.

The last section of the book, chapter 6, "Sunset and Return to the Self: Resolution of Jung's Late-Life Crisis," represents Jung's return to the integrity of the Eternal Way. Jung retired in 1947, at the age of seventy-two, and spent nearly all of his time at his hermitage in Bollingen. Three years later, he wrote the foreword to *The I Ching*, which had also been translated by Wilhelm. In 1951, Jung published his research on synchronicity. After his wife died in 1955, when Jung was eighty, he wrote "Mandalas" and *Mysterium Coniunctionis* (his magnum opus), and meaningfully completed his work on Bollingen and other active imagination projects in stone. During the last few years of his life, Jung finally was achieving harmony between his psyche and Nature. When he was eighty-four, he began work with Aniela Jaffé to complete his autobiography, *Memories, Dreams, Reflections*. In the third and last part of the *opportunity* pictograph, 釁, the ego-Self (and the self-Self) axis or connection is clearly established and the individual (repeated as a smaller version in the left lower quadrant) guards the frontier to consciousness and enlightenment, which is similar to Jung retreating to his Bollingen Tower.

Confucius, who was influenced by Lao Tzu (author of the *Tao Te Ching*), maintained that there were three universal virtues: courage, wisdom, and humanity. Confucius, like Jung in his concept of individuation, affirmed that individual good was incomplete if it did not serve society. Jung actualized the Confucian virtues by giving so much to our world. However, in the final stage of life, Jung turned to and lived out these Taoist virtues:

contentment, enlightenment, and peace. He knew this could only be achieved by taking no action that would interfere with Nature's course. In the end, he realized the ego must be renounced and there must be a return to the integrity-full Self or the great Eternal Way—the Tao.

How Will This Book Help Us to Live in Today's World?

Increasingly, in the West, people find themselves despondent and demoralized because of a lack of purpose and faith. There is a crisis in spirituality and a search for meaning. The dramatic rise in the pollution of our sacred earth and our souls, the marked escalation in violence, and the waning of integrity are evidence of this moral crisis. In Chinese, as we have discussed, crisis is represented by the two pictographs: *danger* and *opportunity*. Hence, even in the most difficult of times, there is the possibility for creative growth and development. Both Taoism and Jung's psychology acknowledge the possibility for constructive change in the midst of chaos, but the responsibility for this constructive change resides with the individual. Taoism and Jungian psychology also share the view that it is only through a transformation of our own psyches that we truly can change ourselves and society in a mature and spiritual way.

In the West, there are both an expanding interest in Jung's psychology and a continuing enchantment with Eastern ideas and values. Taoism, as a branch of Eastern spiritual thought, has grown in popularity. The Taoist sacred text, the *Tao Te Ching*, is the most widely translated book in the world after the *Holy Bible*. Why this burgeoning and synchronous interest in Jung's psychology and Taoist philosophy? I believe it is because they both address the crisis of spirituality and meaning in our lives.

The *Tao Te Ching* was written by Lao Tzu in the sixth century B.C. Lao Tzu was an older contemporary of Confucius (sixth and fifth centuries B.C.) The *Tao Te Ching* drew on even more ancient

Taoist wisdom from *The I Ching (Book of Changes)*, thought to be at least another thousand years older. *Tao* has been interpreted as "the Way"; *Te* has been rendered as "integrity"; whereas *Ching* has been translated as "classic book." Hence, the *Tao Te Ching* is the classic book concerning the Way of integrity. It is both the philosophical and religious text of Taoism. In the fourth and third centuries B.C., Chuang Tzu (or, as it is sometimes spelled, Chuang Tsu) elaborated and popularized Lao Tzu's Taoist work.

Twenty-five hundred years later, Jung's psychology reveals many parallels with Taoism. This is clearly seen in the collaborative work *The Secret of the Golden Flower* (1929) by Wilhelm and Jung. The following examples illustrate some of the similarities between Taoism and Jung's psychology: the world of opposites as manifested by yin/yang, dark/light, shadow/persona, evil/good, and feminine/masculine; the Great Mother as the origin of all things; *The I Ching* and synchronicity, the Tao and the Self; and the Way of integrity and individuation.

Jung stated that

Taoism formulates psychological principles which are of a very universal nature. . . . The great and almost insurmountable difficulty consists in the question of the ways and means to induce people to make the indispensable psychological experiences that open their eyes to the underlying truth. The truth is one and the same everywhere and I must say that Taoism is one of the most perfect formulations of it I ever became acquainted with.[4]

Taoist philosophy is embodied in both the life and work of Carl Jung. Jung left the ego-dominated personal unconscious world of Freud and plunged into the depths of the psyche's collective unconscious. Jung confronted his shadow, contacted his inner wise old man and anima (soul), and through a connection with the Self underwent a transformation. He shed his false self of

"Jung the Freudian" and let his true self emerge. Jung accomplished his own immersion into the natural world of the psyche by accessing his dreams, retreating into solitude, undergoing spiritual experiences, and exploring his creative imagination through painting, writing, sculpting, and building his hermitage at Bollingen. In this book, I use Jung's anecdotes, aphorisms, passages from his books, letters, and his artwork to illustrate how the mysterious Tao guided his growth and development.

Although in despair after leaving Freud, Jung glimpsed the light of the Self in the dark chaos of the collective unconscious. Through a process of transcending the opposites, a metamorphosis transpired. The consummate Jung then crossed over the abyss of meaninglessness and began a new phase of his life with direction and purpose.

The Tao of Jung regards spirituality as the primary ordering principle in psychology. The essential task in analytical (Jungian) psychology is individuation, a process toward wholeness, which like Taoism is characterized by accepting and transcending opposites. The basic tenets of Jung's psychology are also central to Taoism: the downfall of the prime ego position and a rekindling of humility in the face of the Self occur as one proceeds along the Eternal Way of the Tao.

This book offers a way of bridging Eastern and Western spiritual views. It also reveals how ancient Taoist wisdom and Jung's psychology can facilitate movement along one's path toward spiritual wholeness.

The Tao of Jung is by no means a definitive biography. It is also not a treatise on Jung's psychology. Nor is it a detailed spiritual text. But the reader will become better acquainted with both Jung and the Tao through the experience of reading this small volume. By the end of this book, it will be apparent that Jung's psychology (and the individuation process) is virtually the same as the Taoist Way of Integrity. Both come about by letting go of ego and surrendering to the Self or the Tao.

It is the thesis of *The Tao of Jung* that we, too, can let go of ego, confront shadow, and be guided by the soul and spirit. Like Jung before us, we can learn to accept the Tao and flow with life and its inherent ups and downs. Eventually, we can adopt a middle position free of previous excesses and extremes. We can surrender to the natural way of integrity. Jung's life and work illustrate how one person did this, and there is a way for each of us to initiate such an individuation process. With humble egos and our true self identities, we can make a renewed commitment to be creative and serve not only ourselves, but Mother Earth and the whole human family as well.

Part One

Pre-Freud

and Freud

Chapter 1

Sunrise to the Eve of Pubescence:

Becoming a Separate Individual

It is not I who create myself, rather I happen to myself.[1]

CARL JUNG

An individual life is only a brief moment in time; existentially, each person is like a mayfly, here for a day and then gone. Hence, I will use an ancient Egyptian archetypal symbol for birth: the sunrise.

Carl Gustav Jung emerged out of the dark sea of the Self and the Tao on July 26, 1875, in Kesswil, Switzerland, on Lake Constance, and his light began to shine. He embodied and lived the *why* of life: "As far as we can discern, the sole purpose of human existence is to kindle a light in the darkness of mere being."[2]

As Jung says in his *Memories, Dreams, Reflections,* "The story of a life begins somewhere, at some particular point we happen to remember."3 Jung's autobiography starts in Laufen, Switzerland, where his father assumed the same position—as minister of the parish church—that he had held in Kesswil.

Jung's earliest memory is in Laufen, which is near the Rhine Falls and across from Schaffhausen. It is a remembrance of total harmony.

I am lying in a pram, in the shadow of a tree. It is a fine, warm summer day, the sky blue, and golden sunlight darting through green leaves. The hood of the pram has been left up. I have just awakened to the glorious beauty of the day, and have a sense of indescribable well-being. I see the sun glittering through the leaves and blossoms of the bushes. Everything is wholly wonderful, colorful, and splendid.4

The sunrise is like the sunset. Here is Jung at the age of eighty-four (two years before his death), experiencing his infancy again by recalling such a lovely first memory. Jung awakens to "glorious beauty" and a sense of "indescribable well-being." After reading this passage, we can understand Lao Tzu's admonition: "Become as a little child once more."5 Chuang Tzu had an apt view on such quiet receptivity: "There is happiness in stillness. . . . If you are open to everything you see and hear, and allow this to act through you, even gods and spirits will come to you."6

A couple of years later (see plate 1), Jung reports another memory regarding a visit to Lake Constance.

I could not be dragged away from the water. The waves from the steamer washed up to the shore, the sun glistened on the water, and the sand under the water had been curled into little ridges by the waves. The lake stretched away and away into the distance. This expanse of water was an inconceivable pleasure to me, an incomparable splendor. At that

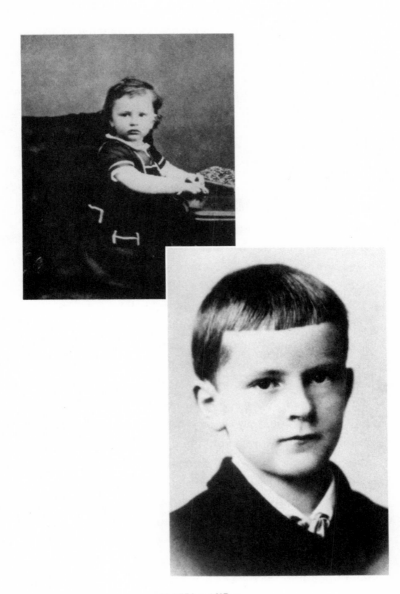

PLATES 1 AND 2.
Jung as a toddler and as a boy

time the idea became fixed in my mind that I must live near
a lake; without water, I thought, nobody could live at all.7

Already, as a boy of three or four, Jung has the Taoist sense of
the symbolic value of water. As Lao Tzu posits, "The supreme
good is like water, which nourishes all things without trying
to. . . . Thus it is like the Tao."8

Jung, as a boy (see plate 2), was also drawn to the opposite:

I was fond of playing with fire. In our garden there was an
old wall built of large blocks of stone, the interstices of which
made interesting caves. I used to tend a little fire in one of
the caves . . . a fire that had to burn forever. . . . My fire
alone was living and had an unmistakable aura of sanctity.9

In addition, as a boy of seven or eight, Jung acted as if consciousness were contained in an inanimate object, that is, a stone
in his garden. Often, when he was alone, he sat on this stone and
a Taoist or Zen-like koan would go through his mind.

"I am sitting on top of this stone and it is underneath." But
the stone also could say "I" and think: "I am lying here on
this slope and he is sitting on top of me." The question then
arose: "Am I the one who is sitting on the stone, or am I the
stone on which *he* is sitting?" This question always per-
plexed me, and I would stand up, wondering who was what
now. The answer remained totally unclear, and my uncer-
tainty was accompanied by a feeling of curious and fascinat-
ing darkness. But there was no doubt whatsoever that this
stone stood in some secret relationship to me. I could sit on
it for hours, fascinated by the puzzle it set me.10

This recollection of the stone memory by Jung is similar to
Chuang Tzu's butterfly dream.

Once upon a time, I, Chuang Tzu, dreamed I was a butterfly flying happily here and there, enjoying life without
knowing who I was. Suddenly, I woke up and I was indeed
Chuang Tzu. Did Chuang Tzu dream he was a butterfly, or
did the butterfly dream he was Chuang Tzu? There must be
some distinction between Chuang Tzu and the butterfly.
This is a case of transformation.[11]

Thirty years later (1912–13), when Jung was going through the
break with Freud and a period of major transformation, he returned to the place where his stone was located. Jung had this
amazing experience:

Suddenly I was again the child who had kindled a fire full of
secret significance and sat down on a stone without knowing whether it was I or I was it. I thought . . . of my life in
Zürich, and it seemed alien to me, like news from some remote world and time. This was frightening, for the world of
my childhood in which I had just become absorbed was *eternal,* and I had been wrenched away from it and had fallen
into a time that continued to roll onward, moving farther
and farther away.[12]

Lao Tzu clarifies the eternal and how it relates to the Tao.

The Tao is infinite, eternal. Why is it eternal? It was never
born: thus it can never die.[13]

As a boy of nine, out of a sense of disunion with himself, Jung
carved a little person out of wood. He colored him black with ink,
dressed him, and together with a blackish stone from the Rhine
(painted with watercolors to have an upper and a lower half) put
him in a small pencil case, which he hid in the attic. Periodically,
Jung secretly stole up to the attic and opened the case and looked

at his manikin and his stone. Jung states, "Each time I did this I placed in the case a little scroll of paper on which I had previously written something ... in a secret language of my own invention."[14] Only later did Jung realize that "the manikin was a little cloaked god of the ancient world, a Telesphoros such as stands on the monuments of Asklepios and reads to him from a scroll."[15]

Late in life, Jung again carved in stone a Telesphoros figure. It is one of the four faces of the famous carved stone at Bollingen (see Plate 3). Meaningfully, Jung had recollected the stone in the pencil case when he was thirty-five years old and working on the beginning of the book, *Symbols of Transformation*, that would lead to his break with Freud. Jung states:

> I read about the cache of soul-stones near Arlesheim, and the Australian *churingas*. I suddenly discovered that I had a quite definite image of such a stone. ... It was oblong, blackish and painted into an upper and lower half.[16]

PLATE 3.
Telesphoros (Front face of Bollingen Stone)

All these stone memories led Jung to muse, "I had a vague sense of relationship between the 'soul-stone' and the stone which was also myself."[17]

Crisis Point: To Be or Not to Be

The crisis point in this stage of Jung's life occured when Jung was eleven and revolved around his fainting spells that resulted from a fall. Jung's head had hit a curbstone after he was pushed down by another boy. He almost passed out. Jung remembered, "At the moment I felt the blow the thought flashed through my mind: 'Now you won't have to go to school anymore.'"[18] Jung used these spells to avoid going to school or doing homework that was brought to his house. This worked for over six months. Jung was taken to numerous doctors and there was a growing consensus that he suffered from epilepsy. Jung overheard his father talking to a friend about his illness and its possible incurability. This was the alarm that woke Jung up.

> From that moment on I became a serious child. . . . Suddenly I felt better than I had in all the months before. And in fact the attacks did not recur. From that day on I worked over my grammar and other schoolbooks every day. A few weeks later I returned to school, and never suffered another attack, even there. The whole bag of tricks was over and done with! That was when I learned what a neurosis is. . . . I saw clearly that I myself had arranged this whole disgraceful situation. . . . Those days saw the beginnings of my conscientiousness, practiced not for the sake of appearances, so that I would amount to something, but for my own sake. . . . What had led me astray during the crisis was my passion for being alone, my delight in solitude. Nature seemed to me full of wonders, and I wanted to steep myself in them. . . . I immersed myself in nature.[19]

About this same time, Jung had a profound experience of what he later termed "ego consciousness."

> I was taking the long road to school from Klein-Hüningen, where we lived, to Basel, when suddenly for a single moment I had the overwhelming impression of having just emerged from a dense cloud. I knew all at once: now I am *myself!* It was as if a wall of mist were at my back, and behind that wall there was not yet an "I." But at this moment *I came upon myself.* Previously I had existed, too, but everything had merely happened to me. Now I happened to myself. Now I knew: I am myself now, now I exist. Previously, I had been willed to do this and that; now I willed.[20]

These passages from Chuang Tzu relate to Jung's experience from a Taoist perspective:

> Do not force things. . . . Can you afford to be careless? So then, flow with whatever may happen and let your mind be free; stay centered by accepting whatever you are doing. This is the ultimate. How else can you carry out your task? It is best to leave everything to work naturally, though this is not easy.[21]

> What is acceptable is acceptable; what is not acceptable is not acceptable. A path is formed by walking on it. . . . When there is a separation, there is coming together. When there is a coming together, there is dissolution. All things may become one, whatever their state of being. Only he who has transcended sees this oneness. He has no use for differences and dwells in the constant. To be constant is to be useful. To be useful is to realize one's true nature. Realization of one's true nature is happiness.[22]

The Tao and the Self

In actuality, the Tao and the Self are unknowable, nameless, and beyond words. However, attempts have been made to know, name, and describe them.

The Tao has been called "the Way," "God," "the Word," "Logos," "the secret," "eternity," "wholeness," "meaning," "celestial mind," "Naturalness," "the essence," "the primal spirit," "the primal real unity," and "ultimate non-being."[23]

The Self has been described as "the central archetype," "life's goal," "the center and totality of the whole psyche," "conscious and unconscious" (in contrast to ego as the center of consciousness), *"imago Dei"* (image of God), and "Supreme Being" (as contrasted with the self, which is the personal being).[24]

It is noteworthy that both the Tao and the Self are symbolized by the circle,[25] no beginning and no end, or the mandala (figure I.I), which means "magic circle" in Sanskrit.

The ego, or ordinary mind, is what develops after we are born. In part, it comes from inside but mostly from the outside—through our interactions with our parents, significant others, and our environment. We introject parts of them, which becomes a false self that gets enmeshed with our true self.

FIGURE 1.1.
Mandala

Part of the task in Taoism and Jung's psychology, on the way to integrity, is to let go of ego and kill the false self so that our true self will emerge. In the empty darkness, we will see the light if we just endure. Our true self is always in a secondary and humble position to the Tao or Self.

Jung writes about his first and second personalities, of which he was aware at an early age. Jung's No. 1 personality is what we would call his persona (mask), ego-image, and ego-identity molded by his parents and society. His No. 2 personality is an ancient source of wisdom from the archetypal collective unconscious, which we will discuss in chapter 2 as it relates to Jung's "early-life crisis" and its resolution.

Chapter 2

Puberty to Psychiatry:

Resolution of Jung's Early-Life Crisis

The mountain [cliff], is of mysterious significance. Here, in the seed, in the deep-hidden stillness, the end of every thing is joined to a new beginning. Death and life, dying and resurrection—these are the thoughts awakened by the transition from the old . . . to the new.[1]

THE I CHING

Jung's adolescence dawned with an experience that harked back to his harmonious first memory. However, this time during the birth of his true self, Chuang Tzu's words would ring true: "The birth of a man, is the birth of his sorrow."[2]

Jung recollects:

One fine summer day . . . I came out of school at noon and went to the cathedral square. The sky was gloriously blue, the day one of radiant sunshine. The roof of the cathedral glittered, the sun sparkling from the new, brightly glazed tiles. I was overwhelmed by the beauty of the sight, and thought: "The world is beautiful and the church is beautiful, and God made all this and sits above it far away in the blue sky on a golden throne and . . ." Here came a great hole in my thoughts, and a choking sensation. I felt numbed, and knew only: "Don't go on thinking now! Something terrible is coming. . . . the most terrible sin."[3]

Jung agonized for three days and two nights and blocked the thoughts about what was coming. Then the dam began to break:

On the third night, however, the torment became so unbearable that . . . I awoke from a restless sleep . . . and felt my resistance weakening. . . . "Now it is coming! . . . *I must think.*"[4]

Being unable to resist any longer, Jung says:

I gathered all my courage, as though I was about to leap forthwith into hell-fire, and let the thought come. I saw before me the cathedral, the blue sky. God sits on His golden throne, high above the world—and from under the throne an enormous turd falls upon the sparkling new roof, shatters it, and breaks the walls of the cathedral asunder.[5]

Jung felt enormous relief, not the expected damnation. He thought he had been tested by God. Jung had seen a dark side to God, and he wondered:

Why did God befoul His cathedral? That, for me, was a terrible thought. But then came the dim understanding that God could be something terrible. I had experienced a dark and terrible secret. It overshadowed my whole life, and I became deeply pensive. . . . It induced in me an almost unendurable loneliness. My one great achievement during those years was that I resisted the temptation to talk about it with anyone. Thus the pattern of my relationship to the world was already prefigured: today as then I am a solitary, because I know things and must hint at things which other people do not know, and usually do not even want to know.[6]

Jung added this secret to two other secrets. One we have discussed in chapter 1, his Telesphoros manikin, who was imbued with "a supply of life-force, the oblong stone."[7] The other was his dream, at age three or four, of a huge phallus in an underground temple,[8] which he did not disclose until he was sixty-five.[9]

Regarding the Christian Church, Jung felt that he did not belong:

> My sense of union with the Church . . . was shattered. . . . I could no longer participate in general faith, but found myself involved in something inexpressible, in my secret, which I could share with no one.[10]

Jung knew to be silent from a very early age, and he maintained this stance through adolescence, which is quite remarkable. He was unknowingly protecting himself and his vulnerable, secret "Other" (No. 2) personality, which will be discussed shortly. Lao Tzu's admonition is apt here: "He who knows does not speak."[11]

Jung's mother later told him that she recalled that he was often depressed during and after his cathedral-shattering experience. Jung says:

> It was not really that; rather, I was brooding on the secret. At such times it was strangely reassuring and calming to sit on my stone. Somehow it would free me of all my doubts. Whenever I thought that I was the stone, the conflict

ceased. "The stone has no uncertainties, no urge to communicate, and is eternally the same for thousands of years," I would think, "while I am only a passing phenomenon which bursts into all kinds of emotions, like a flame that flares up quickly and then goes out." I was but the sum of my [self] emotions, and the Other in me was the timeless, imperishable stone [or Self].[12]

No. 1 and No. 2 Personalities

During Jung's adolescent years, he became distinctly aware that he had two personalities: No. 1 and No. 2. Later, he described it this way:

Somewhere deep in the background I always knew that I was two persons. One was the son of my parents, who went to school and was less intelligent, attentive, hard-working, decent and clean than many other boys. The other was grownup—old, in fact—skeptical, mistrustful, remote from the world of [people], but close to nature, the earth, the sun, the moon, the weather, all living creatures, and above all close to the night, to dreams, and to whatever "God" worked directly in him. . . . it seemed to me that the high mountains, the rivers, lakes, trees, flowers, and animals far better exemplified the essence of God than [people] with their ridiculous clothes, their meanness, vanity, mendacity, and abhorrent egotism—all qualities with which I was only too familiar from myself, that is, from personality No. 1, the schoolboy of 1890. Besides his world there existed another realm, like a temple in which anyone who entered was transformed and suddenly overpowered by a vision of the whole cosmos, so that he could only marvel and admire, forgetful of himself. Here lived the "Other," who knew God as a hidden, personal, and at the same time suprapersonal secret. . . . At such times I *knew* I was worthy of myself, that I was my true self. As soon as I was alone, I could pass into this state. I therefore sought the peace and solitude of this "Other," personality No. 2. . . . In my life No. 2 has been of prime importance, and I have always tried to make room for anything that wanted to come to me from within.[13]

The origin of persona, ego-image, and ego-identity—that is, the No. 1 personality—and the shadow or unconscious "Other"—that is, the No. 2 personality—goes back to Jung's figuring this out as a fifteen-year-old.

The persona is a mask that is used to relate to and interact with the outer world. Usually, the persona is opposite to the shadow. For example, a woman who is overly sweet and angelic on the surface might tend to have a sour and cruel shadow. An illustration from literature is Robert Louis Stevenson's well-known Dr. Jekyll and Mr. Hyde doubling, a single individual with the persona of a wonderful doctor and the shadow of a devilish criminal. As these two examples imply, the persona is often a self-adopted role based on the norms, traditions, ideals, and values of the collective or culture. This is one manifestation of Jung's No. 1 personality. The opposite (the shadow) is always present in the unconscious, and it will express itself one way or another.

The ego (I or me), as Jung characterizes it, is the center of consciousness. In discussing the development of an ego-identity, James Hall introduces the term "ego-image," which could be described as a self-portrait that changes as we grow and develop. Hall explains: "What is 'healthy' for one dominant ego-image at a particular stage of life may be decidedly unhealthy for the nascent ego-image of the next stage of life."[14] The ego is concerned with personal image and identity, and therefore the self (one's personal being). Both the ego and self are secondary to the Self (the Supreme Being) or the Tao. The Self (or Tao) is associated with the dark shadow and the No. 2 personality. Jung's adolescent awareness of his own dual nature mirrors ancient Taoist knowledge, here conveyed by Lao Tzu:

Darkness within darkness.
The gateway to all understanding.[15]

In contrast to Freud, Jung saw the unconscious as collective as well as personal. Hence, the shadow would have both aspects. The personal shadow is that which is repressed, unknown, and evil about oneself. It is typically projected onto other people and usually represented by same-sexed figures in dreams. Jung saw the shadow as "a negative ego-personality" that included "all those qualities we find painful or regrettable."[16] James Hall describes it as "that dark alter ego."[17]

The shadow has also been described as having negative and positive poles.[18] Don Sandner and John Beebe see the shadow as having destructive and constructive parts, both essential to meaningful growth and development.

From another but related vantage point, Erich Neumann defines shadow as

the unknown side of the personality, . . . [which] normally encounters the ego, the center and representative of the light side and of consciousness, in the form of a dark, uncanny figure of evil—to confront whom is always a fateful experience for the individual.[19]

He continues:

At first, the figure is experienced externally as an alien and an enemy, but in the course of its progressive realization in consciousness it is . . . recognized as a component of one's personality. Yet when the personal shadow has been assimilated, the *archetypal* [collective unconscious] *shadow* (in the form of the Devil or Adversary) still remains potent in the psyche.[20]

Lao Tzu speaks of a comparable polarity, which, as we shall see, the young Jung unknowingly embraced.

Honor is a great evil like persona. The reason I experience great evil is that I have a persona. If I have no persona: What evil could I experience?[21]

Jung clearly had a persona (his No. 1 personality), but now he had the insight that it was related to his shadow. As he states:

Naturally I compensated my inner insecurity by an out-ward show of security, or—to put it better—the defect compensated itself without the intervention of my will. That is, I found myself being guilty and at the same time wishing to be innocent.[22]

Jung's sense of his No. 1 personality being guilty stemmed from a troubled home environment. His parents' marriage was problematic from his earliest years. He recalled this from the time he was three. Jung recounts:

I was suffering . . . from general eczema. . . . My illness . . . must have been connected with a temporary separation of my parents. My mother spent several months in a hospital in Basel, and presumably her illness had something to do with the difficulty in the marriage. . . . I was deeply troubled by my mother's being away. From then on, I always felt mistrustful when the word "love" was spoken. The feeling I associated with "women" was for a long time that of in-nate unreliability. "Father," on the other hand, meant reliability and—powerlessness. That is the handicap I started off with. Later . . . I have trusted men friends and been disappointed by them, and I have mistrusted women and was not disappointed.[23]

The family maid, when Jung was between six months and four years of age, was different. She took care of Jung while his mother was away. As Jung says:

She had black hair and an olive complexion, and was quite different from my mother. . . . All this seemed to me very strange and yet strangely familiar. It was as though she belonged not to my family but only to me . . . This type of girl later became a component of my anima.[24] The feeling of strangeness which she conveyed, and yet of having known her always, was a characteristic of that figure which later came to symbolize for me the whole essence of womanhood.[25]

This dark-skinned maid saved his life when Jung, as a three- or four-year-old, was

crossing the bridge over the Rhine Falls to Neuhausen. The maid caught me just in time—I already had one leg under the railing and was about to slip through. These things point to an unconscious suicidal urge or, it may be, to a fatal resistance to life in this world.[26]

The possibility of having "a fatal resistance to life in this world" relates directly to another recollection when Jung was a young medical student: "It seemed to me miraculous that I should not have been prematurely annihilated."[27]

Jung's reflections on his early years in the house in Klein-Hüningen, near Basel, involved many frightening memories.

My parents were sleeping apart. I slept in my father's room.
All sorts of things were happening at night, things incomprehensible and alarming. From the door to my mother's
room came frightening influences. At night Mother was
strange and mysterious. One night I saw coming from her
door a faintly luminous, indefinite figure whose head de-
tached itself from the neck and floated along in front of it, in
the air, like a little moon. . . . This process was repeated six
or seven times.[28]

If this was not scary enough, when Jung was seven years old, he
remembered:

I was sick with pseudo-croup, accompanied by choking fits.
One night during an attack I stood at the foot of the bed,
my head bent back over the bed rail, while my father held
me under the arms. Above me I saw a glowing blue circle
about the size of the full moon, and inside it moved golden
figures which I thought were angels. This vision was repeated, and each time it allayed my fear of suffocation. But
the suffocation returned in anxiety dreams. I see in this a
psychogenic factor: the atmosphere of the house was beginning to be unbreathable.[29]

Could the presence of the moon have a double meaning? His
mother was suffering from "lunacy," and already his No. 1 personality was yielding to No. 2, so he would be comforted by the
moon or yin (the archetype of the feminine). According to Lao
Tzu: "It turns in a circle and does not endanger itself. One may
call it 'the Mother of the World.' I do not know its name. I call it
Tao."[30]
Perhaps these troubling early visions were premonitions or
guiding images based on ancient Chinese wisdom of what was to
unfold in Jung's life:

Without beginning, without end,

Without past, without future.

A halo of light surrounds the world of law.

We forget one another, quiet and pure, altogether powerful
and empty.

The emptiness is irradiated by the light of the heart and of
heaven.

The water of the sea is smooth and mirrors
The moon in its surface.

The clouds disappear in blue space; the mountains shine
clear.

Consciousness reverts to contemplation;
The moon-disk rests alone.[31]

Confrontation with Father and Authority

When Jung was fifteen, he was very conflicted about his father. As
Jung puts it:

> There arose in me profound doubt about everything my fa-
> ther said. When I heard him preaching about grace, I always
> thought about my own experience. What he said sounded
> stale and hollow. . . . I wanted to help him, but I did not
> know how. Moreover, I was too shy to tell him of my
> experience [the secrets] . . . [and] I was afraid to wield that
> authority which my "second personality" inspired in me. [32]

By the time Jung was eighteen (see plate 4), he had had many discussions with his father, but they did not turn out well. As Jung says:

> [These talks] irritated [my father], and saddened him. "Oh
> nonsense," he was in the habit of saying, "you always want
> to think. One ought not to think, but believe." I would
> think, "No, one must experience and know."[33]

PLATE 4.
Jung at seventeen

Jung anticipated great things transpiring when he had the experience of his confirmation and communion: "the pinnacle of religious initiation." His father, as parson, was in charge of the event. However, it failed and "nothing at all had happened."[34]

Jung expands on further trouble with his father:

> I was seized with the most vehement pity for my father. All at once I understood the tragedy of his profession and his life. . . . An abyss had opened between him and me, and I saw no possibilities of ever bridging it.[35]

However, Jung described some positive moments with his father. These were few but extremely meaningful. During Jung's summer holidays when he was fourteen, he was sent, on doctor's orders, to Entlebuch for a cure; he had a fitful appetite and was in poor health. At the end of his stay, Jung's father came and got him and then gave him "the best and most precious gift . . . ever."[36]

His father bought him a ticket on a cogwheel railway that went from Vitznau to the top of a towering mountain called the Rigi. Jung's father said, "You can ride to the peak alone. I'll stay here, it's too expensive for the two of us. Be careful not to fall down anywhere."37

Jung then stood on top of the Rigi,

> in the strange thin air, looking into unimaginable distances. "Yes," I thought, "this is it, my world, the real world, the secret, where there are no teachers, no school, no unanswerable questions, where we can *be* without having to ask anything?" I kept carefully to the paths, for there were tremendous precipices all around. It was all very solemn, and I felt one had to be polite and silent up here, for one was in God's world. Here it was physically present.38

As an adolescent, Jung already had the ancient Taoist sense of Tao (God) expressed by Chuang Tzu:

> How vast, how invisible
> This coming-to-be!39

And:

> Tao is Great in all things
> Complete in all, Universal in all
> [Tao] causes being and non-being
> But is neither being nor non-being.40

And an even older wisdom of Lao Tzu:

> So the learning of complete people is to return their essential nature to non-being and float their minds in spaciousness.41

As a teenager, Jung seemed to know what the first Chinese Taoist master meant, when he talked about the Ultimate Authority:

The Way is to straighten oneself and await the direction of destiny.[42]

And Lao Tzu also said,

Find out destiny,
govern mental functions,
make preferences orderly,
and suit real nature.[43]

Here are Jung's own words:

From the beginning I had a sense of destiny, as though my life was assigned to me by fate and had to be fulfilled. This gave me an inner security, and, though I could never prove it to myself, it proved itself to me. *I* did not share this certainty, *it* had me. Nobody could rob me of the conviction that it was enjoined upon me to do what God wanted and not what I wanted. That gave me the strength to go my own way. Often I had the feeling that in all decisive matters I was no longer among men, but was alone with God. And when I was "there," where I was no longer alone, I was outside time; I belonged to the centuries; and He who then gave answer was He who had always been, who had been before my birth. He who always is was there. These talks with the "Other" [No. 2 personality] were my profoundest experiences: on the one hand a bloody struggle, on the other supreme ecstasy.[44]

More About God: The Ultimate Authority

Proceeding down his path during preuniversity days, Jung pondered a great deal about God. His idea that "God has a personality and is the ego of the universe"[45] was the seed of a later and extremely creative and provocative work, *Answer to Job*.[46] In *Answer to Job*, it is Jung's thesis that God wanted to become human. Why else would he have tormented Job so, and then later have died on the cross as Jesus?

Jung also mused that

> it was not at all unreasonable to suppose that God . . . intended to create a world of contradiction . . . and life meant simply being born to die.[47]

Lao Tzu corroborated this last thought of Jung's, but he phrased it differently: "A person comes fresh to life and enters into death."[48] Chuang Tzu said it even more simply: "Easy come, easy go."[49]

Jung continued questioning, as any bright, open, thoughtful, and creative adolescent would:

> The "wonderful harmonies" of natural law looked to me more like chaos tamed by fearful effort. . . . I either did not see or gravely doubted that God filled the natural world with [only] His goodness. This, apparently, was another of those points which must not be reasoned about but must be believed. In fact, if God is the highest good, why is the world, His creation, so imperfect, so corrupt, so pitiable? "Obviously it has been infected and thrown into confusion by the devil," I thought. But the devil, too, was a creature of God.[50]

Lao Tzu's wisdom in describing the Tao (God) parallels Jung's adolescent insight:

... the One
This is called the formless form,
the objective image.
This is called the darkly chaotic.[51]

Similarly, Lao Tzu's words also affirm Jung's intuitive pubescent knowledge:

When everyone knows goodness,
this accounts for badness.[52]

Often Jung was silent and reserved to the point of depression. Then Jung recorded a change:

Between my sixteenth and nineteenth years the fog ... lifted, and my depressive states of mind improved. No. 1 personality emerged more and more distinctly.[53]

Nevertheless, Jung

was filled with conflicting thoughts. . . . No. 1 wanted to free himself from the pressure or melancholy of No. 2. It was not No. 2 who was depressed, but No. 1 when he remembered No. 2. It was just at this time that, out of the clash of opposites, the first systematic fantasy of my life was born. [54]

Jung's fantasy, which was alchemical, involved a well-fortified castle with a water tower, which was his home. It was simple and there were no fine halls. He had a laboratory in the cellar. Jung made gold out of a mysterious substance that copper roots drew from the air.[55]

This active imagination of Jung's was prophetic regarding his study of both Chinese Taoist and European alchemy. Jung spent many years working on transforming his psychological state of lead to gold.[56]

The University Years: Natural Science and Medicine

Jung based his decision to study natural science on two dreams.

> In the first dream I was in a dark wood that stretched along the Rhine. I came to a little hill, a burial mound, and began to dig. After a while I turned up, to my astonishment, some bones of prehistoric animals. This interested me enormously, and at that moment I knew: I must get to know nature, the world in which we live, and the things around us.
>
> Then came a second dream. Again I was in a wood; it was threaded with watercourses, and in the darkest place I saw a circular pool, surrounded by dense undergrowth. Half immersed in the water lay the strangest and most wonderful creature: a round animal, shimmering in opalescent hues, and consisting of innumerable little cells, or of organs shaped like tentacles. It was a giant radiolarian. . . . It aroused in me an intense desire for knowledge, so that I awoke with a beating heart.[57]

In the context of focusing on natural science, Jung had a sudden inspiration to study medicine. It represented a way to integrate science, which Jung felt met the needs of his No. 1 personality, and the humanities (primarily philosophy—particularly Kant, Schopenhauer, Swedenborg, and Goethe), which benefited his No. 2 personality.[58] Clearly, these interests and those of archaeology and spirituality had a lot to do with his eventual specialization in psychiatry and particularly in psychoanalysis.

Ironically, before Jung's formal entrance into the University of Basel, his father was reading Freud's translation of Bernheim's book on suggestion and its therapeutic value.[59] However, Jung noted that "[my father's] psychiatric reading made him no happier. His depressive moods increased in frequency and intensity as did his hypochondria."[60]

Jung's father became quite ill just when Jung entered the university. Given Jung's unique affinity with stones, it is noteworthy that his father complained of having "stones in the abdomen." Tragically, he became bedridden in the fall of 1895. He died early in 1896 at the age of fifty-four, when Jung was just twenty years of age. A few days after his father's death, as if she wanted him dead, his uncanny mother made this eerie comment: "He died in time for you." Jung interpreted this to mean: "You did not understand each other and he might have become a hindrance to you."[61] The whole experience of losing his father was traumatic, but as Jung tells it:

> The words "for you" hit me terribly hard, and I felt that a bit of the old days had now come irrevocably to an end. At the same time, a bit of manliness and freedom awoke in me. After my father's death I moved into his room, and took his place inside the family. For instance, I had to hand out the housekeeping money to my mother every week, because she was unable to economize and could not manage money.[62]

The Shadow and Father Complex

Jung was set up for a *father complex* in that his No. 2 personality provided him with a father archetype (with both positive and negative aspects). Jung's complicated and strained relationship with his father, plus his father's early death, precipitated a *negative father complex,* which took Jung nearly all of his life to resolve. The *negative father,* on both the personal (No. 1) and archetypal (No. 2) levels, is also related to the *shadow* (male figures in dreams and projections onto relationships with men). Jung had an early experience with the shadow in a dream that both "frightened and encouraged" him.

It was night in some unknown place, and I was making slow and painful headway against a mighty wind. Dense fog was flying along everywhere. I had my hands cupped around a tiny light which threatened to go out at any moment. Everything depended upon my keeping this little light alive. Suddenly I had the feeling that something was coming up behind me. I looked back, and saw a gigantic black figure following me. But at the same moment I was conscious, in spite of my terror, that I must keep my little light going through the night and wind, regardless of all dangers. When I awoke I realized that the figure was . . . my own shadow on the swirling mists, brought into being by the little light I was carrying. I knew too, that this little light was my consciousness, the only light I have. My own understanding is the sole treasure I possess, and the greatest. Though infinitely small and fragile in comparison with the powers of darkness, it is still a light, my only light.

This dream was a great illumination for me. Now I knew that No. 1 was the bearer of light, and that No. 2 followed him like a shadow. . . . I must go forward against the storm. . . . In the role of No. 1, I had to go forward—into study, moneymaking, responsibilities, entanglements, confusions, errors, submissions, defeats. The storm pushing against me was time, ceaselessly flowing into the past, which just as ceaselessly dogs our heels. It exerts a mighty suction which greedily draws everything living into itself; we can only escape from it—for a while—by pressing forward. The past is terribly real and present, and it catches everyone who cannot save his skin with a satisfactory answer.[63]

Again, early in his life, Jung was aware of No. 1 being his persona and ego-image and that No. 2 was clearly his shadow. Jung's insight (from his light of ego consciousness) enabled him to realize something Lao Tzu knew long ago:

> To see the smallest means to be clear.
> To guard wisdom means to be strong.
> If one uses one's light
> in order to return to this clarity
> one does not endanger one's person.
> This is called the hull of eternity.[64]

Choosing Psychiatry as a Specialty

Predetermining, in a real way, Jung's choice of psychiatry was his decision in 1898 to investigate "So-called Occult Phenomena" for his doctoral thesis in medicine. As Jung says:

> All in all, this was the one great experience which wiped out all my earlier philosophy and made it possible for me to achieve a psychological point of view. I had discovered some objective facts about the human psyche. Yet the nature of the experience was such that once again I was unable to speak of it. I knew no one to whom I could have told the whole story. Once more I had to lay aside an unfinished problem. [65]

After he began to read a psychiatric text by Krafft-Ebing, his future vocational choice was settled. Jung says:

> The author called the psychoses "diseases of the personality." My heart suddenly began to pound. I had to stand up and draw a deep breath. My excitement was intense, for it had become clear to me, in a flash of illumination, that for

me the only possible goal was psychiatry. Here alone the two currents of my interest could flow together and in a united stream dig their own bed. Here was the empirical field common to biological and spiritual facts, which I had everywhere sought and nowhere found. Here at last was the place where the collision of nature and spirit became a reality.[66]

What Jung is expressing is an ancient truth about the essence of meaning when he makes his lifelong task the unification of the opposites of nature (yin) and spirit (yang). It puts him clearly on the Taoist Eternal Way as well as establishes the core of his psychology.

On December 10, 1900, Jung started in his new position in psychiatry as assistant to a well-known psychiatrist and kind father-surrogate, Eugen Bleuler, at the Burghölzli Mental Hospital, Zürich.

Echoing Lao Tzu's ancient words, "If you don't study sincerely, you won't listen to the Way deeply,"[67] Jung says:

For six months I locked myself within the monastic walls [of the Burghölzli] in order to get accustomed to the life and spirit of the asylum, and I read through the fifty volumes of the *Allegemeine Zeitschrift für Psychiatrie* from its very beginning, in order to acquaint myself with the psychiatric mentality.[68]

The above passage speaks to Jung's immersion into psychiatry as a spiritual and in-depth experience. He also says, "I need scarcely mention that my concentration and self-imposed confinement alienated me from my colleagues."[69]

Without a doubt, the two foremost Taoist masters, Lao Tzu and Chuang Tzu, would have understood and supported Jung's journey. For example, Chuang Tzu states:

He goes his way
Without relying on others
And does not pride himself
On walking alone.[70]

Unlike his father, Jung stood on the mountain cliff and chose the authority of Nature, to remain orientated to the sky but connected to the earth. Also unlike his father, who died early, Jung would live a long life by pursuing not only his path but also that of the ancient Way.

However, let us remember that Jung's father gave his son the ticket to the mountaintop—to the cliff's edge. And he told his son to be careful. What Jung found there is reminiscent of this passage from Chuang Tzu:

[The] Tao [Self]
Is simplicity, stillness,
Indifference, purity.
Here the highest knowledge
Is unbounded.[71]

Nevertheless, Jung's conflict with his father foreshadowed the *father complex* and authority problem that came into play in his relationship with Freud.

Chapter 3

The Freud Years:

Emergence of Jung's Mid-Life Crisis

The "personal complex" casts its shadow on all purely logical thought! [1]

SIGMUND FREUD

Because of his father's death when Jung was only twenty, he filled in as surrogate father for his younger sister, who was then eleven; and, unconsciously, as a surrogate husband for his mother. There were also economic problems and some pressure for Jung to drop out of the university and get a job. To his credit, Jung persisted down his own path. He borrowed money from an uncle and lived at home until age twenty-five, when he completed his medical education at the University of Basel.

Once Jung left Basel for Zürich and his assistantship at the Burghölzli in Zürich, he never returned to Basel. He also never again lived under the same roof as his mother. Nevertheless, it was difficult to leave. As Jung recounts:

> For my mother it was hard that I was leaving Basel. But I
> knew I could not spare her this pain, and she bore it
> bravely.[2]

Jung had to make a break from his mother in order to become his
own person. Of course, this takes repeated effort, and the son must
eventually do battle with the mother in order to establish his own
life. Barbara Hannah reports how Jung "woke up to this fact."[3]

> His mother came into his room one day where there were a
> lot of diagrams pinned up on the wall. She looked at them
> disparagingly and remarked: "I suppose you think those are
> something." She shattered her son by this contempt, for he
> had poured a lot of creative energy into them and he felt
> they had thrown some light onto a dark question. For two
> or three days, he told us, he was totally unable to work, ut-
> terly lamed in the vital sphere of his creativeness. Then he
> pulled himself together and thought: "She knows nothing
> about it and I shall not let her interfere whatever it leads to,
> whatever it costs her." Immediately his creativeness was
> freed and he was able to continue with his diagrams and thus
> to clarify his problem.[4]

This incident helped Jung to know that he had to leave the
nest.

Ironically, his mother also helped him to glimpse his nonma-
ternal anima,[5] which was another way she unconsciously helped
him to leave her. When Jung was twenty-one, shortly after his father's death, he was on his way to visit a classmate and friend who
lived in Schaffhausen. Jung's mother asked him, while there, to
stop in and see Frau Rauschenbach. When they had lived in
Laufen, the future Frau Rauschenbach, who was a friend of Jung's
father, had taken care of Jung as a little boy.

This was what Jung records about Bertha Schenk (who later became Frau Rauschenbach):

> From the period of my parent's separation I have another memory image: a young, very pretty and charming girl with blue eyes and fair hair is leading me, on a blue autumn day, under golden maple and chestnut trees along the Rhine below the Falls, near Wörth castle. The sun is shining through the foliage, and yellow leaves lie on the ground. This girl later became my mother-in-law. She admired my father. I did not see her again until I was twenty-one years old.[6]

Now let us return to Jung's account of his visit to the Rauschenbach home:

> As I entered the house I saw a girl about fourteen years with braids standing on the stairs. I knew at once: this is my wife. I was deeply moved. Though I had seen her but a moment, I immediately knew and with absolute certainty that she would become my wife.
>
> Still today, I remember exactly that I told that to my school friend directly afterwards. Of course, he simply laughed at me. I said to him, "Just laugh, but you will see."[7]

It is noteworthy that in his autobiography, Jung recalls Emma's mother as a young girl, but when she was with Jung in Laufen, when he was one to four years old, she would have been between twenty and twenty-three. Jung mentions her immediately after discussing his attachment to the dark-skinned young maid who he says was an anima figure for him. Surely, Emma's mother and Emma were also anima figures for him. To know, and only at a glance, that a teenage girl would become his wife would have to be close to 100 percent anima projection! Whereas, Jung was standing in for his father at home, he was clearly breaking away from him, his mother, and Frau Rauschenbach by displacing and projecting pure anima onto Emma. Of course, in the normal development of the anima, a man is expected to break away from his mother and to have a romantic love of his own.

In 1902, when Jung was twenty-seven and in an independent position, he returned to ask for Emma's hand in marriage. Initially, she refused him, but Emma's "no" soon became a "yes."[8] Perhaps she sensed the anima projection at first and only agreed to marry when Jung began to see Emma as herself. They were married in 1903 (see plate 5), and for their first six years together they were obliged to live in a flat at the Burghölzli. The newlyweds unconsciously adhered to ancient Taoist words of wisdom:

PLATE 5.
Wedding portrait: Carl and Emma Jung

When husband and wife mate, clouds and rain form in the secret room. In a year they give birth to a child and each rides on a crane.9

Their first child, Agathe, was born in 1904, one year after they married. Subsequently, while living at the Burghölzli, Gret and Franz were born in 1906 and 1908, respectively.

Freud: The First Encounter

When Freud's *The Interpretation of Dreams* was published in 1900, Jung read it immediately. However, as he says, "I had laid the book aside, at the time, because I did not yet grasp it. At the age of twenty-five I lacked the experience to appreciate Freud's theories."10

However, Jung grasped enough of Freud's theories to report on *The Interpretation of Dreams* to a staff meeting on January 25, 1901 (this was at the request of Eugen Bleuler, the director of the Burghölzli Mental Hospital) and to cite this work in his doctoral dissertation, which was published in 1902.11

In 1903, Jung felt he fully grasped Freud's magnum opus. As he says:

I once more took up *The Interpretation of Dreams* and discovered how it all linked up with my own ideas. What chiefly interested me was the application to dreams of the concept of the repression mechanism. . . . This was important to me because I had frequently encountered repression in my experiments with word association; in response to certain stimulus words the patient either had no associative answer or was unduly slow. . . . such a disturbance occurred each time the stimulus word had touched on a psychic lesion or conflict. . . . the repressive mechanism was at work here.12

In 1906, Jung sent Freud a copy of his book *Diagnostic Association Studies*, which supported Freud's theory of repression. Freud responded in April 1906 with a short letter of thanks, thus initiating a correspondence between these two pioneers of psychoanalysis that would last until their formal break in January 1913.

From the start, Jung had a religious devotion to Freud that also mirrored Freud's position. Freud came to view their relationship in this way:

> If I am Moses, then you are Joshua and will take possession of the promised land of psychiatry, which I shall only be able to glimpse from afar.[13]

In one of Jung's first letters to Freud, he uses religious terminology: "Bleuler is now completely converted."[14]

In December 1906, Jung sent Freud his book *The Psychology of Dementia Praecox*, and in the foreword he stated, "I am indebted to the brilliant discoveries of Freud."[15] However, even in this foreword, Jung expresses reservations about Freud's sexual theory. Jung states:

> If I, for instance, acknowledge the complex mechanisms of dreams and hysteria, this does not mean that I attribute to the infantile sexual trauma the exclusive importance that Freud apparently does. Still less does it mean that I . . . grant [sexuality] the psychological universality which Freud . . . postulates.[16]

The First Meeting with Freud

Freud invited Jung to visit him in Vienna and Jung did so on Sunday, March 3, 1907.[17] Regarding this historic meeting, Jung says:

We met at one o'clock in the afternoon and talked virtually without pause for thirteen hours. Freud was the first man of real importance I had encountered; in my experience up to that time, no one else could compare with him. . . . I found him extremely intelligent, shrewd, and altogether remarkable. And yet my first impressions of him remained somewhat tangled; I could not make him out.[18]

While Jung was impressed with what Freud said about his sexual theory, he felt Freud's words "could not remove [his] hesitations and doubts."[19] This represented an echo of Jung's troubled relationships with his own father, who also did not want Jung to doubt but to believe.

In addition, Jung was troubled by Freud's view of spiritual matters. He says, "Above all, Freud's attitude toward the spirit seemed . . . highly questionable. . . . [Any] expression of spirituality [he saw as] repressed sexuality."[20]

Despite these reservations, Jung defended Freud at professional meetings and in his scholarly writings. Freud let Jung know how much he appreciated this but recommended, "In my opinion, attack is the best form of defense."[21]

Jung became an ardent Freudian and his No. 1 personality deferred to Freud, the father-like authority, who appeared to know the "truth." At first, Jung's No. 1 personality led him to doubt himself rather than Freud. For example, Jung says, "It is possible that my reservations about your far-reaching views are due to my lack of experience."[22] Thus, although Jung had sensed already that there were to be problems adhering to Freud's views and following him, these reservations were based on ancient wisdom to be found eventually in his own repressed No. 2 personality and in the words of Lao Tzu:

To use the mind for purposes of pride and aggrandizement is like a gusty wind or a violent storm; it cannot last long.[23]

Chuang Tzu said:

That is what men call judgment, decision.
Their pronouncements are as final
As treaties between emperors.
O, they make their point!
Yet their arguments fall faster and feebler
Than dead leaves in autumn and winter.
Their talks flow out like piss,
Never to be recovered.
They stand at last, blocked, bound, and gagged,
Choked up like old drain pipes,
The mind fails. It shall not see light again.[24]

In his commentary on a new translation of *The Secret of the Golden Flower*, Thomas Cleary says:

The conscious mind (which does the thinking) is supposed to be a servant of the original mind [the Tao or spirit], but the activity of the conscious mind tends to become so self-involved that it seems to have become an independent entity. When "the sword is turned around" . . . the original mind retrieves command over the delinquent conscious mind.[25]

In light of the above three passages, these words of Freud, addressed to Jung, take on new meaning.

As you know, I suffer all the torments that can afflict an "innovator"; not the least of these is the unavoidable necessity of passing, among my own supporters, as the incorrigibly self-righteous crank or fanatic that in reality I am not. Left alone for so long with my ideas, I have come, understandably enough, to rely more and more on my own deci-

sions. In the last fifteen years I have been increasingly im-
mersed in preoccupations that have become monotonously
exclusive. . . . This has given me a kind of resistance to being urged to accept opinions that differ from my own.[26]

Lao Tzu would have diagnosed Freud's problem as narrowness:

It is only after the Way narrows that it concedes to knowledge. . . . When knowledge is allowed to take over, there is
disturbance in the mind.[27]

Lao Tzu also outlined the prescriptive treatment: "Detach from
intellectual knowledge . . . and return to clarity and calm,"[28]
which is something Jung did in his later years.

In a real way, the following passage from *The Secret of the
Golden Flower* further predicts what will transpire with Jung in the
future.

The life of the spirit comes from the prior death of the
mind. If people kill the mind, the original comes alive.
Killing the mind does not mean quietism, it means undi-
vided concentration.[29]

In his commentary, Cleary quotes from *The Book of Balance and
Harmony*:

Of old it has been said, always extinguish the stirring mind
[ego], don't extinguish the shining mind [Self]. The unstir-
ring mind is the shining mind, the mind that does not stop is
the wandering mind.[30]

The main problem that led to Jung's break with Freud was
Freud's insistence that his sexual theory was the "truth." As Jung
recalls:

There was no mistaking the fact that Freud was emotionally involved in his sexual theory to an extraordinary degree. . . . I had a strong intuition that for him sexuality was a sort of *numinosum*. This was confirmed by a conversation that took place . . . (in 1910).

Freud said to me, "My dear Jung, promise me never to abandon the sexual theory. That is the most essential thing of all. You see, we must make a dogma of it, an unshakable bulwark." He said that to me with great emotion, in the tone of a father saying, "And promise me this one thing, my dear son: That you will go to church every Sunday." In some astonishment I asked, "A bulwark against what?" To which he replied, "Against the black tide of mud"—and then he hesitated for a moment, then added—"of occultism." First of all, it was the words "bulwark" and "dogma" that alarmed me; for a dogma, . . . an undisputable confession of faith, is set up only when the aim is to suppress doubts once and for all. But that no longer has anything to do with scientific judgment; only with a personal power drive.

This was the thing that struck at the heart of our friendship. I knew I would never be able to accept such an attitude. What Freud seemed to mean by "occultism" was virtually everything that philosophy and religion . . . had learned about the psyche. To me the sexual theory was just as occult, that is to say, just as unproved an hypothesis, as many other speculative views. As I saw it, a scientific truth was a hypothesis which might be adequate for the moment but was not to be preserved as an article of faith for all time.[31]

My conversation with Freud had shown me that he feared that the numinous light of his sexual insight might be extinguished by a "black tide of mud." Thus a mythological situation had arisen: the struggle between light and darkness. That explains its numinosity, and why Freud immediately fell back on his dogma as a religious means of defense.[32]

Freud did adhere to the following statement by Lao Tzu, but Jung eventually stopped this type of fruitless action:

To let knowledge produce troubles, and then use knowledge to prepare against them, is like stirring water in hopes of making it clear.[33]

Freud did not, but Jung eventually did actualize these wise words of Lao Tzu: "Knowing unconsciously is best; presuming to know what you don't know is sick."[34]

The Death of Jung the Freudian

Freud was convinced as early as 1909 that Jung wanted to kill him. Most likely this was in part true for both men. Freud must have projected his desire to be killed onto Jung. After all, in the end, Freud had his internist kill him on command with two lethal injections of morphine.[35]

Symptomatic of Freud's death wish was the fact that he fainted twice in Jung's presence. The first occasion was in 1909, when they were in Bremen about to sail for America to give their Clark University Lectures. Freud collapsed when Jung was talking about the "peat bog corpses" that are to be found near Bremen. The second fainting episode occurred during the 1912 Psychoanalytic Congress in Munich. As Jung tells it:

Someone had turned the conversation to Amenophis IV (Ikhnaton). The point was made that as a result of his negative attitude toward his father he had destroyed his father's cartouches on the steles, and that at the back of his great cre-

ation of a monotheistic religion there lurked a father complex. This sort of thing irritated me, and I attempted to argue
that Amenophis had been a creative and profoundly religious
person whose acts could not be explained by personal resis-
tances toward his father. On the contrary, I said, he had held
the memory of his father in honor, and his zeal for destruction had been directed only against the name of one god
Amon, which had been everywhere annihilated. . . .

At that moment Freud slid off his chair in a faint. . . . I
picked him up, carried him into the next room, and laid him
on a sofa. As I was carrying him, he half came to, and I shall
never forget the look he cast at me. In his weakness he
looked at me as if I were his father. Whatever other causes
may have contributed to this faint—the atmosphere was
very tense—the fantasy of father-murder was common to
both cases.

At the time Freud frequently made allusions indicating
that he regarded me as his successor. These hints were em-
barrassing to me, for I knew that I would never be able to
uphold his views properly, that is to say, as he intended
them.[36]

Likewise in 1909, Freud had maintained:

It is remarkable that on the same evening that I formally
adopted you as an eldest son, anointing you as my successor
and crown prince,—*in partibus infidelium* [in the lands of the
unbelievers]—. . . you should have divested me of my pater-
nal dignity.[37]

Freud grandiosely claims to be Jung's father and a king who
can anoint Jung as his successor and crown prince. It took Jung
three years to convince himself that he had to let go of his No. 1
Freudian personality and kill off his false self. No wonder Freud

felt Jung wanted to kill him, but actually it was to be the death of Jung the Freudian.

The boat trip to America—likewise in 1909—proved to be decisive. Freud and Jung analyzed each other's dreams, and one occasion revealed the depth of differences between them. As Jung reports:

> I interpreted [the dream] as best I could, but added that a great deal more could be said about it if he would supply me with some additional details from his private life. Freud's response to these words was a curious look—a look of utmost suspicion. Then he said, "But I cannot risk my authority!" At that moment he lost it altogether. That sentence burned itself into my memory and in it the end of our relationship was already foreshadowed. Freud was placing personal authority above trust.[38]

Many years later—after Freud's death—Jung revealed that this dream involved Freud's illicit relationship with his wife's sister.[39] On a visit to Freud before the 1909 trip to the United States, Minna (Freud's wife's sister) had disclosed to Jung a difficult triangular relationship involving her intimate relationship with Freud, and she had asked him for help. Apparently, Jung was prepared to help, but his attempts only backfired, producing deep repercussions, which subsequently altered the course and development of psychoanalysis.

The trickster in Jung then got in the act. Again on the 1909 boat trip to America, Jung shared his multi-level house dream with Freud. The dream, forerunner of Jung's theory of the collective unconscious, ended in a stone cave deep in the earth. There Jung found the remains of a primitive culture and two human skulls that were very old and half-disintegrated. Freud wanted to know about the two skulls. Whose were they? Jung answered (knowing that Freud did not know he knew about Freud's difficult situation), "My wife and my sister-in-law."[40] Jung's response was a somewhat veiled jab of a thorn into Freud's side.

The critical piece of creativity, precipitating the break with Freud, was Jung's book *The Psychology of the Unconscious* (later revised and retitled, *Symbols of Transformation*). The creation of this work involved a transformation of the destructive death energy related to Jung's false (Freudian) self into his true self. However, prior to the completion of this book, Jung was blocked for months on the chapter entitled "The Sacrifice." Despite his wife saying otherwise, Jung knew that his relationship with Freud would end once he completed this major work, which challenged Freud's sexual theory. In a real sense, Jung's sacrifice of his Freudian ego-identity was a prelude for his becoming a spiritual being (which is what "sacrifice" means). Jung's death and rebirth experience, that is, a Taoist emptying out, was central to his proceeding along the Way of integrity.

Whereas Freud avoided the darkness, Jung voluntarily entered it full force. Jung's destiny was to enter the Tao, which is the darkness—the mysterious source. As Lao Tzu said:

> The Way says, "In darkness follow
> the authority of Nature . . . [and]
> stand alone in the middle"[41]

Most meaningful are the words of wisdom from *The Secret of the Golden Flower*: "When the dark is at rest, the light begins to move."[42] And from Jung's commentary on this Taoist work: "Darkness gives birth to light."[43] Jung was on his way, and the Way, as Lao Tzu said:

> It is not up to another, but up to oneself; it is not up to anyone but the individual. When the individual attains it, everything is included.[44]

Part Two

Post-Freud

Chapter 4

Creative Illness

Resolution of Jung's Mid-Life Crisis

When I parted from Freud, I knew that I was plunging into the unknown. Beyond Freud, after all, I knew nothing; but I had taken the step into darkness. [1]

CARL JUNG

Darkness within darkness
The gateway to all understanding. [2]

LAO TZU

Following the final break from Freud, Jung courageously began to live what was to become the core of his psychology: death of the false self and birth of the true self. Meaningfully, during Advent—precisely on December 12, 1913—Jung experienced symbolic death. This is how Jung described it:

> I resolved upon the decisive step. I was sitting at my desk once more, thinking over my fears. Then I let myself drop.

Suddenly it was as though the ground literally gave way beneath my feet, and I plunged down into dark depths. I could not fend off a feeling of panic. But then, abruptly, at not too great a depth, I landed on my feet in a soft, sticky mass. I felt great relief, although I was apparently in complete darkness. After a while my eyes grew accustomed to the gloom, which was rather like a deep twilight. Before me was the entrance to a dark cave, in which stood a dwarf with a leathery skin, as if he were mummified. I squeezed past him through the narrow entrance and waded knee deep through icy water to the other end of the cave where, on a projecting rock, I saw a glowing red crystal. I grasped the stone, lifted it, and discovered a hollow underneath. At first I could make out nothing, but then I saw that there was running water. In it a corpse floated by, a youth with blond hair and a wound in the head. He was followed by a gigantic black scarab and then by a red, newborn sun, rising up out of the depths of the water. Dazzled by the light, I wanted to replace the stone upon the opening, but then a fluid welled out. It was blood. A thick jet of it leaped up, and I felt nauseated. It seemed to me that the blood continued to spurt for an unendurably long time. At last it ceased, and the vision came to an end.[3]

Jung had boldly chosen to fall into the dark morass of the collective unconscious: the shadowy world beyond the conscious ego. The opportunity for rebirth is symbolized by the dark cave, which represents the womb. In his way is a dwarf with leathery skin, but Jung squeezes by. The mummified dwarf symbolizes an old ego-identity that had to die. In Indian mythology, Shiva steps on a dwarf that represents the ego when this deity does its creative dance of death and rebirth. Jung bravely picks up a glowing red crystal, which reveals a hollow with water (often symbolizing the

Tao) running through it. Then Jung sees a dead blond male youth with a head wound, which represents the ambitious Jung as a Freudian who was wounded in the head and couldn't think, or be, for himself. The corpse, followed by the gigantic scarab and then a red, newborn sun emerging out of the water is clearly a death-rebirth motif. Dazzled by the luminosity, Jung tried to replace the red crystal, but he saw more red: blood spurted out, continuing for a long time. Blood represents death as well as life. The fact that the blood kept *coming and coming* indicates that there will be additional experiences of symbolic death and new life for Jung in the future.

This was Jung's own reaction and interpretation:

> I was stunned by this vision. I realized, of course, that it was a hero and solar myth, a drama of death and renewal, the rebirth symbolized by the Egyptian scarab. At the end, the dawn of a new day should have followed, but instead came that intolerable outpouring of blood—an altogether abnormal phenomenon, so it seemed to me.[4]

The last sentence is telling; more of Jung's blood must flow. It also becomes potentially more violent and sickening.

Egocide and Transformation

Six days later, on December 18, 1913, Jung went through a suicidal crisis and underwent what I would call "egocide."[5] So that now "seeing red" or experiencing anger had turned into murderous rage. Jung dreamed that he teamed up with a dark-skinned savage and they shot and killed Siegfried. When he awoke, a voice within him said, "You *must* understand the dream . . . at once! . . . If you do not understand [it], you must shoot yourself!"[6] Jung tells us that he was frightened because in the drawer of his night table lay a loaded revolver. Fortunately for him, and us, Jung committed egocide, not suicide. Jung realized, "The dream showed that the attitude embodied by Siegfried, the [German] hero, no longer suited me. Therefore, it had to be killed."[7] Hence, Jung and his "primitive shadow" psychically murdered this negative aspect of Jung's ego-image and identity. Of course, Siegfried also sounds like Sigmund, which affirms that this is a killing of the heretofore dominant Freudian ego-image or Jung's *false self*.

After this dream, Jung says that "new forces were released in me which helped me to carry the experiment with the unconscious to a conclusion."[8]

Jung went deeper into the depths of the inner space. He described five "steep descent[s]"[9] in these ways: "I found myself at the edge of a cosmic abyss"; "It was like a voyage to the moon"; "[I descended] into empty space"; "[I went to] the land of the dead"; and "[I traveled to] the other world."[10]

When Jung left Freud, he became the master of his own fate. Jung surrendered his ego based on his Freudian false self. The Self (or Tao), a force beyond the ego, became the guide to his *true self*.

Lao Tzu cautions us to not overesteem great men. Jung had done this vis-à-vis Freud. As Jung's No. 1 personality died, his No. 2 personality or wise old man (the "archetype of meaning")[11] emerged from within. Lao Tzu calls this wise old man figure the Master.

Now in Lao Tzu's words:

The Master leads
by emptying people's minds
and filling their cores,
by weakening their ambition
and toughening their resolve.
He helps people lose everything

they know, everything they desire,
and creates confusion
in those who think that they know.[12]

Lao Tzu continues:

The Tao is like a well:
used but never used up.
It is like the eternal void:
filled with infinite possibilities.[13]

Hold on to the center.[14]

During one of these descents into the dark depths of his collective unconscious, Jung encountered "an old man with a white beard" who said he was Elijah.[15] Jung's Elijah was with Salome, a "beautiful young girl" who was blind. Jung called them a "strange couple" who had a black serpent living with them that had an attraction for him. Jung saw a parallel with Lao Tzu and the dancing girl.[16] Jung felt "distinctly suspicious" of Salome and he "stuck close to Elijah because he seemed to be the most reasonable of the three [with] a clear intelligence."[17] Jung saw Elijah as "the figure of the wise old prophet," and Salome as a blind anima figure as "she does not see the meaning of things."[18]

Out of the Elijah figure developed Philemon. Jung said, "Philemon was a pagan and brought with him an Egypto-Hellenistic atmosphere with a Gnostic coloration."[19]

Philemon: Jung's Taoist Master

Jung first encountered Philemon in a dream as a winged being that appeared from the right and sailed across the blue sky (see plate 6). He described this figure as:

an old man with the horns of a bull. He held a bunch of four keys, one of which he clutched as if he were about to open a lock. [Philemon] had the wings of the kingfisher with its characteristic colors.[20]

Jung acknowledged:

I did not understand this dream-image, [so] I painted it in order to impress it upon my memory. During the days when I was occupied with the painting, I found in my garden, by the lake shore, a dead kingfisher! I was thunderstruck, for kingfishers are quite rare in the vicinity of Zürich and I have never since found a dead one. The body was recently dead—at the most, two or three days—and showed no external injuries.[21]

PLATE 6.
Image of Philemon

As Jung said:

> Philemon represented a force which was not myself. . . . I held conversations with him, and he said things which I had not consciously thought. . . . He said I treated thoughts as if I generated them myself, but in his view thoughts were like animals in the forest, or people in a room, . . . and [he] added, "If you should see people in a room, you would not think that you had made those people, or that you were responsible for them." It was he who taught me psychic objectivity, the reality of the psyche.[22]

At this time, Jung was concerned that he might lose himself in a bottomless abyss. He maintained, "My ego felt devalued."[23]

Assuming Philemon represents an inner Taoist Master leading to the Tao, these reflections of Chuang Tzu clearly apply:

> The true men of old were not afraid
> When they stood alone in their views.
> They had no mind to fight Tao.
> They did not try, by their own contriving,
> To help Tao along.
> These are the ones we call true men.
> Minds free, thoughts gone
> All that came out of them
> Came quiet, like the four seasons.[24]

At least Jung's No. 2 personality, represented by Philemon, was not frightened. Jung had an inner security in his psychic Taoist Master. As Lao Tzu says:

> The Tao doesn't take sides;
> it gives birth to both good and evil.[25]

Hence, an evil figure came into Jung's consciousness out of the mysterious source. Jung describes what happened:

> Later, Philemon became relativized by the emergence of yet another figure, whom I called Ka . . . [whose] expression [had] something demonic about it—one might also say, Mephistophelian.[26]

We will discuss the implications of this figure in a later section.

Evolution of Jung's Anima

Jung's anima figure, Salome, was blind. She was with Elijah, the only Jewish prophet in the Old Testament to ascend to heaven with the promise to return, clearly representing a spirit force connected to the Supreme Being. Jung embodied something of a religious father figure even at a young age. For instance, when he was at the gymnasium, his schoolmates had nicknamed him "Father Abraham." Jung reflected on this at the time: "No. 1 could not understand why, and thought it silly and ridiculous. Yet somewhere in the background I felt that the name had hit the mark."[27]

The reason for this early patriarchal orientation was that Jung, unknowingly at first, embodied an inner authority, No. 2 personality (Father Abraham), which he sought externally (as we saw in the preceding chapter) in the Moses figure of Freud.

In the context of an increasingly strained relationship with Freud, Jung's blind anima was projected in the context of his own negative father complex. In 1911, Jung (aged thirty-six) started seeing a new twenty-three-year-old patient named Antonia (Toni) Wolff. She was brought to see Jung by her mother, because Toni was extremely depressed after the sudden death of her father. A positive and powerful father transference evolved into an erotic transference. Jung terminated the analysis in 1914 and subsequently was involved in an intimate relationship with his former patient. Jung blindly projected the love of the feminine aspect of the psyche (his blind Salome figure) onto Toni Wolff. Jung's concept of the anima (the feminine part of a man's psyche) was discovered through this "acting out" behavior and all three—Jung, Toni, and Jung's wife, Emma—contained and eventually accepted this neurotic triangle. This is not to take away from the intense jealousy and suffering that must have been experienced by these two women. The Jung children also must have found it to be a confusing and difficult situation. In addition, it was a troubling predicament for Jung, but he felt he would go mad without both women in his life.

Jung was clearly out of balance with a mistress and a wife. As Chuang Tzu says:

Too much pleasure? Yang has too much influence.
Too much suffering? Yin has too much influence.[28]

Lao Tzu was also clear about the need for balance between the two opposing forces, which he characterized as yin (dark, passive, feminine) and yang (light, active, and masculine). He said, "Of the energies of the universe, none is greater than harmony. Harmony means the regulation of yin and yang."[29]

Jung needed to be on a balanced middle path, that is, the way of transcendence (understanding and insight). However, he first had to give sight to his inner Salome figure, his anima or feminine side. In order to catalyze this process, Jung found himself creating images, that is, drawing or painting figures in his dreams and visions. He asked himself:

"What am I really doing? Certainly this has nothing to do with science. But then what is it?" Where upon a voice within . . . said, "It is art."[30]

This was the voice of another female patient with whom Jung had had an erotic relationship (which predated his involvement with Toni Wolff). He describes her as having a strong transference to him. He wrote, "She had become a living figure in my mind."[31] Although Jung did not disclose this patient's name in his autobiography, she was identified much later as Sabina Spielrein.[32]

Jung actually disagreed with this "inner voice," that is, with Sabina Spielrein, and claimed these creative works were not art, but rather works of "nature."[33] However, what Jung had discovered in working with his images was a new technique that he called "active imagination," which allowed him—and countless others—to express unconscious shadow material as a painted image or as various other creative products (sculpture, dance, poetry, music, etc.), so that it could be effectively dealt with psychologically.

What Jung stumbled upon, blindly at first, was that the potentially destructive "acting out," based on the projection of the feminine aspect of his psyche onto actual women patients, was actually a contrasexual part of his own psyche. As he withdrew these projections, Jung realized the presence of an innovative psychological concept of "inner feminine," anima or soul for himself and other men, and postulated the parallel concept of "inner masculine," animus or spirit for women.[34]

Restoration of Balance

During the post-Freud years of 1913 to 1916, Jung was afraid of losing his mind, and with good reason. He came to the edge of madness, but in doing so, he killed off his false self and emptied out the contents of his Freudian ego-identity. He made mistakes, but he learned from them. For example, the blind Salome regained her sight and the concept of the anima was born. Jung as therapist and analyst helped himself, and in a real way, he embodied the archetype of the "wounded healer." One of the most unique results of his own creative active imagination was the *Septem Sermones ad Mortuos*, which he wrote in 1916.[35] This work is essentially Taoist in that it unifies opposites, which is the hallmark of both this ancient Chinese spiritual philosophy and of Jung's psychology. The *Seven Sermons to the Dead* memorializes the symbolic death of Jung's false self and provides the template for his new life based on his true self.

In "Sermo I," Jung writes of the dead coming back, which most likely represents his return from the land of the dead.

Harken: I begin with nothingness. Nothingness is the same as fullness. In infinity full is no better than empty. Nothingness is both empty and full.

This nothingness or fullness we name the PLEROMA. CREATURA is not in the pleroma, but in itself.

What is changeable, however, is creatura. Therefore [it is] the one thing which is fixed and certain. . . . [36]

The question ariseth: How did creatura originate? . . . The pleroma hath all, distinctiveness and non-distinctiveness.

Distinctiveness is creatura.

If we do not distinguish, we get beyond our own nature, away from creatura. We fall into indistinctiveness, which is the other quality of the pleroma. We fall into the pleroma itself and cease to be creatures. We are given over to dissolution in the nothingness. This is the death of the creature. Therefore we die in such measure as we do not distinguish. Hence the natural stirring of the creature goeth towards distinctiveness, fighteth against primeval, perilous sameness. This is called the PRINCIPIUM INDIVIDUATIONIS. This principle is the essence of the creature.

We must, therefore, distinguish the qualities of the pleroma. The qualities are PAIRS OF OPPOSITES, such as—

The Effective and the Ineffective.
Fullness and Emptiness.
Living and Dead.
Difference and Sameness.

Light and Darkness.

The Hot and the Cold.

Force and Matter.

Time and Space.

Good and Evil.

Beauty and Ugliness.

The One and the Many. [Etc.]

As we are pleroma itself, we also have all these qualities in us. . . . When, however, we remain true to our own nature, which is distinctiveness, we distinguish ourselves from the good and the beautiful, and, therefore, at the same time from the evil and ugly. And thus we fall not into the pleroma, namely into nothingness and dissolution.[37]

Therefore not after difference, as ye think it, must ye strive; but after YOUR OWN BEING. At bottom, therefore, there is only one striving, namely, the striving after your own being.[38]

"Sermo II" deals with God and the devil.

God is not dead. Now, as ever, he liveth. God is creatura, for he is something definite, and therefore distinct from the pleroma.

Effective void is the nature of the devil. God and devil are the first manifestations of nothingness, which we call pleroma. . . . In so far as god and devil are creatura they do not extinguish each other, but stand one against the other as effective opposites.

God and devil are distinguished by the qualities fullness and emptiness, generation and destruction.

We name [god] . . . ABRAXAS.[39]

"Sermo III" is about Abraxas.

Hard to know is the deity of Abraxas. . . . Abraxas [is] life, altogether indefinite, the mother of good and evil.

Abraxas begetteth truth and lying, good and evil, light and darkness.

[Abraxas] is the hermaphrodite of the earliest beginning.

It is abundance that seeketh union with emptiness.

It is holy begetting.

It is love and love's murder.

It is the appearance and the shadow of man.[40]

"Sermo IV" concerns the meaning of the first four numbers.

Four is the number of the principal gods.

One is the beginning, the god-sun.

Two is Eros; for he bindeth twain together and outspreadeth himself in brightness.

Three is Tree of Life, for it filleth space with bodily forms.[41]

"Sermo V" is about spirituality and sexuality.

Spirituality conceiveth and embraceth. It is womanlike and therefore we call it MATER COELESTIS, the celestial mother. Sexuality engendereth and createth. It is manlike, and therefore we call it PHALLOS, the earthly father.

The sexuality of a man is more of the earth, the sexuality of a woman is more of the spirit.

The spirituality of man is more heaven, it goeth to the greater.

The spirituality of a woman is more of the earth, it goeth to the smaller.

Distinctiveness leadeth to singleness. [But] the Gods force you to communion.

Communion is depth.
Singleness is height.
Communion giveth warmth, singleness giveth us light.[42]

"Sermo VI" relates to the demons of sexuality and spirituality.

The daemon of sexuality approacheth our soul as a serpent. It is half-human and appeareth as thought-desire. The daemon of spirituality descendeth into our soul as the white bird. The serpent is an earthly soul . . . a spirit, and akin to the spirits of the dead. The white bird is a half-celestial soul . . . [and] bideth with the Mother.[43]

"Sermo VII" concerns the human being as "gateway."

At immeasurable distance standeth one single Star in the zenith.

In this world is [the individual] Abraxas, the creator and the destroyer of [his/her/] world.

This Star is the god [Supreme Being] and the goal of [the human being].

Prayer increaseth the light of the Star.

[The human being] here, [the Supreme Being] there.

Weakness and nothingness here, there externally creative power.

Here nothing but darkness and chilling moisture. There wholly sun.[44]

Jung's process of unifying opposites expressed in the *Seven Sermons to the Dead* parallels numerous passages from Lao Tzu's *Tao Te Ching*. For instance:

All creatures under heaven are born from being;
Being is born from non-being.[45]

Being and non-being create each other.
Difficult and easy support each other.
Long and short define each other.
High and low depend on each other.
Before and after follow each other.[46]

The Tao is called the Great Mother:
empty yet inexhaustible,
it gives birth to infinite worlds.[47]

Each separate being in the universe
returns to the common source.
Returning to the source is serenity.[48]

The Tao is dark and unfathomable,
How can it make her radiant?
Because she lets it.[49]

If you want to become whole,
let yourself be partial.
If you want to become straight,
let yourself be crooked.
If you want to become full,
let yourself be empty.
If you want to be reborn,
let yourself die.
If you want to be given everything,
give everything up.[50]

Know the male,
Yet keep to the female.[51]

When creation begins,
only then are there names.[52]

Whosoever does not perish in death lives.[53]

The Tao of progress appears as retreat.

The smooth Tao appears to be rough.
The highest purity appears as shame.
The true essence appears to be changeable.[54]
Going out is Life, going in is death.[55]

The world has a beginning:
that is the Mother of the World.[56]

To see the smallest means to be clear.
To guard wisdom means to be strong.
If one uses one's light
in order to return to this clarity
one does not endanger one's person.
This is called the hull of eternity.[57]

Chuang Tzu also embodied the wisdom of the *Seven Sermons to the Dead*:

You have got lost, and are trying
To find your way back
To your own true self.[58]

Great knowledge sees all in one.
Small knowledge breaks down into the many.
When the body sleeps, the soul is enfolded in One.
When the body wakes, the openings begin to function.
Pleasure and rage
Sadness and joy
Hopes and regrets
Change and stability
Weakness and decision
Impatience and sloth:
All are sounds from the same flute,
All mushrooms from the same wet mould.

Day and night follow one another and come upon us
Without our seeing how they sprout![59]

Naturally, the Tao or Self encompasses both Pleroma and
Creatura, which allows Chuang Tzu to sum up the essence:

The pivot of the Tao passes through the center where all af-
firmations and denials converge. [The person] who grasps the
pivot is at the still-point from which all movements and op-
positions can be seen in their right relationship. Hence [the
individual] sees the limitless possibilities of both "Yes" and
"No." Abandoning all thought of imposing a limit or taking
sides. [The true self] rests in direct intuition. Therefore I said:
"Better to abandon disputation and seek the true light."[60]

The Luminous Center

Chuang Tzu knew that "in the deep dark the person alone sees
light."[61]

What contributed to Jung's emergence from the darkness in
1917? Jung outlined two events: (1) breaking off the relationship
with the woman who claimed his active imagination products had
artistic value and (2) creating mandalas.[62] Jung's termination of
his relationship with Sabina Spielrein allowed his anima to see. He
then had more soul energy to put into active imagination. His
anima or muse was searching for a form, clearly this contributed
to Jung's spontaneous creation of his first mandala in 1916 (see
plate 7). During 1918–19, while the commandant of a camp for
British internees, Jung sketched a mandala in a notebook every
morning. He noted that these mandalas corresponded to his psychic state. For example, if Jung was feeling centered, the mandala
appeared balanced, if not, it was unbalanced.

It is noteworthy that the Tao is symbolically represented by a
circle with no beginning or end. Lao Tzu says:

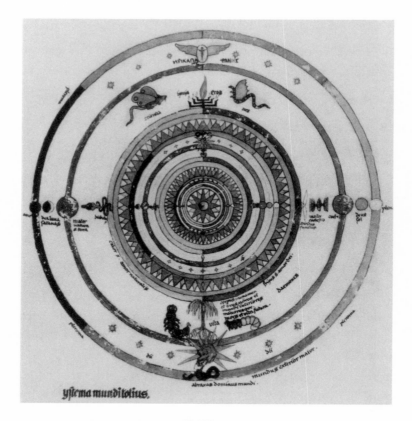

PLATE 7.
Jung's first mandala

There is one thing that is invariably complete.
Before Heaven and Earth were, it is already there:
so still, so lonely.
Alone it stands and does not change.
It turns in a circle and does not endanger it.
One may call it "the Mother of the World."
I do not know its name.
I call it Tao.[63]

Now we know why Jung chose the Sanskrit term "mandala," which means "magic circle." Jung states:

Only gradually did I discover what the mandala really is: "Formation; Transformation, Eternal Mind's eternal recreation."[64] And that is the Self, the wholeness of the personality, which if all goes well is harmonious.[65]

"It became increasingly plain to me," according to Jung, "that the mandala is the center."[66]

Jung sums up his discovery:

During those years, between 1918–1920, I began to understand that the goal of psychic development is the Self. There is no linear evolution; there is only a circumambulation of the Self. Uniform development exists, at most, only at the beginning; later, everything points toward the center. This insight gave me stability, and gradually my inner peace returned. I knew that in finding the mandala as an expression of the Self I had attained what was for me the ultimate. Perhaps someone else knows more, but not I.[67]

Jung had attained the wisdom expressed in Lao Tzu's maxim of twenty-five hundred years earlier: "Just stay at the center of the circle and let all things take their course."[68]

Jung's preoccupation with centering, and with understanding that two halves or four quarters of a circle make a whole, led him to devise psychic typology and to write *Psychological Types*,[69] a personality theory of major import. The backdrop for this discovery was Jung's struggle to discern how his personality type was different from Freud's and then to relate that to their inevitable parting.

Jung first conceived of two attitudes: introversion (I) and extraversion (E). As one might suspect, there was a major difference here: Jung was introverted and Freud extraverted. These attitudes are the yin and yang of how we approach the world; we are primarily either quiet and receptive *or* assertive and expressive (see figure 4.1).

Individuals have an innate predominant attitude or temperament—that is, they are either orientated toward the inner world (I) or the outer world (E). Ideally, people need to become facile with both modes.

Jung then formulated four psychological functions of personality (see figure 4.2). Two functions have to do with *perceiving:* sensation based on the five senses and intuition based on the sixth sense. The other two functions have to do with *processing* the data perceived: thinking based on a logical, cognitive method and feeling based on an affective, evaluative approach.

Imagine the personality of an individual who is consciously extraverted, gathers data in a sensate way, and processes it in a cognitive way (EST). This typological makeup is common and stereotypic of the modern-day person in the West: active (outgoing), perceiving through the five senses (what one sees, hears, smells, tastes, and touches is what is real), and logical in solving problems. Of course, the unconscious shadow is always present

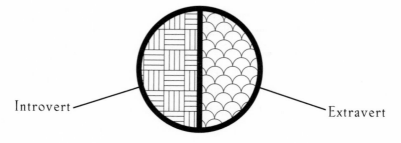

FIGURE 4.1.
Psychological Attitudes

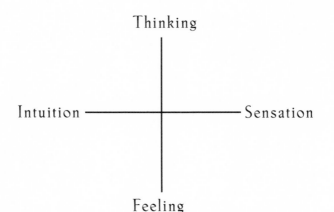

FIGURE 4.2.
Psychological Functions

and forms the basis of the stereotypic kind of person in the East: passive (quiet), perceiving primarily through intuition (the sixth sense), and processing data through evaluative feeling. Historically, the former Western way has been associated with males and the patriarchy and the latter Eastern way with females and the matriarchy. However, this kind of rendering (based on Cartesian dualism) leads to inner battles or neuroses (divided selves), splitting, and in the worst-case scenarios to outer battles or war. The key is to realize that the two are actually one: the Self or Tao, that is, the Way to integrity and lasting peace.

Jung's typology theory represents another way of centering, and it evolved out of his mandalic period (1918–28). The goal of the Self is to promote wholeness, which is the end result of individuation, Jung's developmental theory concerning the way of integrity. Just as the Self contains tension of psychological opposites, Jung saw the aim of Taoism as "deliverance from the cosmic tension of opposites by a return to *Tao*."[70]

In image form (see figure 4.3), this represents a transformation of *t'ai chi* into *wu chi*,[71] or one could call it a regression in the

FIGURE 4.3.
The Transformation of Duality into Wholeness

service of the Tao, Self, or wholeness—that is, back to the primal beginning.

The Tao (like the Self) encompasses all opposites. As Jung maintained, "Tao is the right way, . . . the middle road between opposites, freed from them and yet uniting them in itself."[72]

In his autobiography, Jung summarized his work in typology and how it related to the Tao as follows:

The book on types yielded the insight that every judgment made by an individual is conditioned by his [or her] personality type and that every point of view is necessarily relative. This raised the question of the unity which must compensate this diversity, and it led me directly to the Chinese concept of Tao.[73]

The Bollingen Tower: Putting Down Roots and Branching Out

In 1922, at the age of forty-seven, Jung purchased a piece of "mother earth" that had formerly been part of the nearby monastery of St. Gall. The land was south of the village of Bollingen and on the upper lake of Zürich; Jung said he had "always been drawn by the scenic charm" of this area. As if embodying the essence of this chapter's symbolic part of the opportunity pictograph, Jung was ready to put down his own roots and to begin to branch out. As he says:

Gradually, through my scientific work, I was able to put my fantasies and the contents of the unconscious on a solid footing. Words and paper, however, did not seem real enough to me; something more was needed. I had to achieve a kind of representation in stone of my inner most thoughts and of the knowledge I had acquired. Or, to put it another way, I had to make a confession of faith in stone. That was the beginning of the "Tower," the house which I built for myself at Bollingen.[74]

Reflecting on Jung's objective to be one with stone, I think back to his boyhood union with stone, which he returned to during his troubled adolescence and, again, thirty years later when profoundly depressed after his break with Freud. At Bollingen, Jung's goal to be one with stone speaks to his life-long closeness to Nature and sense of Harmony with the Tao. Related to this theme, I recall a conversation I had with Hayao Kawai, former professor of psychology at Kyoto University and the first Jungian analyst in Japan. He was telling me about "non-personal therapy" and I asked him what he meant by this phrase. He explained: "Westerners are concerned with personal, interpersonal, and transpersonal therapy. What I am talking about is helping the patient to be like a stone." Jung would have understood this immediately. Frances Baruch, in an important article, "Jung and the Stone,"[75] tracks the stone in Jung's life from beginning to end and comments on its meaning from the perspective of a Jungian-oriented sculptor.

Originally, Jung thought he would build a "primitive one-story dwelling . . . a round structure with a hearth in the center . . . [like] an African hut where the fire, ringed by a few stones, burns in the middle, and the whole life of the family revolves around the center."[76] However, as Jung says, "I altered the plan . . . for I felt it was too primitive. . . . So in 1923 the first round house was built."[77]

We all know the feeling of struggling to create something that has not yet come together—a piece of the puzzle is missing. For me, in the writing of this book, my visit to Bollingen provided such a missing piece. I remember walking up to the outer gate with Carl Jung's grandson Peter (who has a reverence for his grandfather and the sacredness of Bollingen). At once, I sensed Jung's achieved harmony with Nature. I could see and feel how Jung had made peace with himself and the forces of Nature. The feeling grew stronger as I entered the fenced-in courtyard and went into the loggia (covered in 1951, with its hand-painted ceiling). When I walked through the huge arched wooden doorway, I felt as though I were entering a tomb (see plate 8). To the left, I stepped through a smaller doorway into the original Tower. The large round room represented Jung's feeling function and it was the cooking area, where the hearth was located (see plate 9). I ventured up the wee stairs and first entered Emma's room, simple and graceful as I imagined she was, with a floral pattern painted around an arched window that opened upon the lake. Next I entered Philemon's room and was awestruck by the huge life-like icon mural on the wall. This peaceful room contained the spirit of Jung's No. 2 personality. Then, I went into Jung's own bedroom, which was the smallest of the three upstairs rooms. He had painted a huge mandala above his bed that was very Oriental and seemed to capture the essence of the Tao. Jung's only son Franz (Peter's father), recalled his father (whom he calls "C.G.") painting this mandala in 1924. White light comes to a center point out of multiple spheres, twelve in a first circle and twenty-four in a second ring. Everything radiates out of a deep azure blue background that seems to be water, which often symbolizes the Tao. The outer four boundaries are red and appear to be flames. This mandala represents the Taoist concept of light (the Secret of the Golden Flower) emanating from the union of water (yin/anima) and fire (yang/animus). I stared at this image for what seemed like an eternity, until Peter finally called out, "Let's go through the

PLATE 8.
Peter Jung opening the main Bollingen doorway.

rest of Bollingen." But my feet would not move. I was anchored. The image had captured me—bound me to the dazzling light at the center of Jung's storm. Here was *the image* of his transcendent function uniting the conscious and unconscious Jung in a Taoist way.

Later, rereading *The Secret of the Golden Flower*, I came to this passage and I nearly fell out of my chair:

Only when [one has] sincere intention in the work . . . [and when] The true purpose is subject to the earth [Bollingen];

PLATE 9.
The original Tower hearth room

the color of the earth is yellow, therefore in books on the
Elixir of Life it is symbolized by the yellow germ. When the
Abysmal [water of the Abyss, *puer aeternus*] and the Clinging
(Li) [fire frequently compared to a bride] unite, the Golden
Flower appears; the golden color is white.

. . . Even as heaven turns about the polar star as a
center point, so among men the right intention must
be master. Therefore the completion of the Elixir of
Life depends entirely on the harmonizing of the right
purpose.

. . . When a person has found the method of making
thoughts and energy harmonize with one another . . . spirit
and energy are pure and clear; the heart is empty, human
nature *(hsing)* manifest, and the light of consciousness trans-
forms itself into the light of human nature. If one continues
to hold firmly the light of human nature, the Abysmal [wa-
ter, *K'an*] and the Clinging (fire, *Li*) have intercourse spon-

taneously. When the Abysmal and the Clinging commingle, the holy fruit is born.[78]

Jung's healing tree had been planted: it was rooted in spiritual ground and its branches would eventually reach far and wide protecting his newfound *Temenos*.

After dwelling in his hermitage at Bollingen, Jung says:

> From the beginning I felt the Tower as in some way a place of maturation—a maternal womb or a maternal figure in which I could become what I was, what I am and will be. It gave me a feeling as if I were being reborn in stone.[79]

Jung had a lifelong "kinship with stone" that was "divine"; he viewed stone as "the bottomless mystery of being, the embodiment of spirit."[80]

Chuang Tzu comments on the tower:

> The spirit has an impregnable tower
> Which no danger can disturb
> As long as the tower is guarded
> By the invisible Protector
> Who acts unconsciously [with the]
> Entire sincerity of Tao
> He will be at peace
> With [people] and spirits
> And will act rightly, unseen,
> In his own solitude,
> In the tower of his spirit.[81]

Aniela Jaffé, who knew Jung extremely well, says:

Nobody really knew Jung who had not been with him in Bollingen. Here his feeling for Nature showed itself in a way it could not do in Küsnacht. . . . It was a genuine rootedness in his own earth, a communion with the whole country-side. . . . But one thing above all gave Bollingen its special quality: silence. Jung was a great one for silence, just as he could on occasion be a torrential talker. The two compensated each other. It was a vital necessity for him to sink himself in profound introversion; this was the fountainhead of helpful and vivifying powers. Creative ideas took shape in the inner and outer stillness.[82]

Lao Tzu says:

Ordinary men hate solitude.
But the Master makes use of it,
embracing his aloneness, realizing
he is one with the whole universe.[83]

Lao Tzu also says of "real people,":

They are full yet appear to be empty.
They govern the inside, not the outside.
Clear and pure, utterly plain, they do
not contrive artificialities but return
to simplicity. [They comprehend] the fundamental,
embracing the spirit,
Seeing the evolution of events, they keep to the source.
Their attention is focused internally, and they
understand calamity and fortune in the context
of unity.
They keep to the simplicity of wholeness
and stand in the center of the quintessential.[84]

As Jung's tree of individuation grew in the soil of Mother Earth, his being at Bollingen enlarged into a stone mandala. Lao Tzu knew of such an essential connection:

The Tao is called Great Mother:
empty yet inexhaustible,
it gives birth to infinite worlds.[85]

Chapter 5

Union of
East and West:

*Emergence of Jung's
Late-Life Crisis*

*The Chinese have never failed to recognize the paradoxes and the po-
larity inherent in what is alive. The opposites always balanced one
another—a sign of high culture. One-sidedness, though it lends mo-
mentum, is a mark of barbarism.*[1]

CARL JUNG

Reflect for a moment on the image representing the fifth stage of
Jung's life. The two sets of cocoons, each pair joined by a thread,
are in balance. It is a time of further opportunity—of quiet inner
growth and development. Despite the peaceful symbol, a change
is in the making: the emergence of Jung's late-life crisis. What
pairs of opposites are contained within these four chrysalises? We
must remember two things: (1) this is a time of incubation (the
caterpillar awaits its metamorphosis into a butterfly, and (2) a quaternity represents a unity (four is three plus one, two plus two, but
ultimately it is one). Henceforth, what fourfold, what double, and
what singular transformation awaits Jung (and us)?

Now that Jung had achieved a certain stability and rootedness both at his home in Küsnacht and at his retreat at Bollingen, it was time for Jung's tree to grow more extensively and branch out significantly. He was adhering to his evolving philosophy of life, that was to find meaning by developing one's full personality, by "saying yea to oneself."[2]

In 1924, at the age of forty-nine, Jung traveled to America, where he visited the Taos pueblos in New Mexico. There he realized that he was still "caught up and imprisoned in the cultural consciousness of the white man."[3] He befriended the chief of the Taos Pueblo Indians, whose name was Ochwiay Biano (Mountain Lake). The chief shared an observation about white people that "struck [a] vulnerable spot" in Jung, and "unveiled a truth to which [he] was blind."[4]

"See," Ochwiay Biano said, "how cruel the whites look. Their lips are thin, their noses sharp, their faces furrowed and distorted by folds. Their eyes have a staring expression; they are always seeking something. What are they seeking? The whites always want something; they are always uneasy and restless. We do not know what they want. We do not understand them. We think that they are mad."[5]

Jung asked Mountain Lake why he thought the whites were all mad. "They say that they think with their heads," he replied. Jung said, "Why of course," and he asked him in surprise. "What do you think with?" The chief indicated his heart.[6]

Mountain Lake had held a mirror up to Jung, and it stunned the visitor from Switzerland. Jung reflected, "I fell into a long meditation. For the first time in my life, so it seemed to me, someone had drawn for me a picture of the real white man."[7]

Hence, one of the pairs of opposites that Jung would have to deal with was: thinking with the head and thinking with the heart. Jung was a heady (intellectual) thinking type, so this would be no easy feat. In fact, it would take a score of years and a near-fatal heart (and soul) attack before Jung could actualize Mountain Lake's wise words in a Taoist way, that is, to think in the way the chief described—with the heart.

Another significant journey, this time to Africa, occurred in the following year, which marked a half century of living for Jung. It is noteworthy that Jung's next adventure took him to a world of blacks. In an uncanny way, it was as if Jung were following Lao Tzu's precept:

> Know the white
> Yet keep to the black:
> be a pattern for the world.
> If you are a pattern for the world,
> the Tao will be strong inside you
> and there will be nothing you can't do.[8]

Black and white became another pair of opposites for Jung to understand and accept; after all, it represented the yin and yang of Taoism and Jung's evolving psychology.

In the autumn of 1925, Jung embarked on a safari to Kenya and Uganda. Jung felt curiously at home in Africa, as if it had been his for "countless millennia."[9] Once on the Athi Plains, a great game preserve near Nairobi, Jung saw a magnificent savanna with

> gigantic herds of animals: gazelle, antelope, gnu, zebra, warthog, and so on. Grazing, heads nodding, the herds moved forward like slow rivers. There was scarcely any sound save the melancholy cry of a bird of prey. This was the stillness of the eternal beginning, the world as it had always been, in the state of non-being.[10]

Again, this time in Africa, Jung and Lao Tzu meet:

We work with being,
but non-being is what we use.[11]

And

All things are born of being.
Being is born of non-being.[12]

Below Mount Elgon, Jung camped among the Elgony. At one point, he met with the *laibon,* the old medicine man, and when Jung

> asked him about his dreams, he answered with tears in his eyes, "In old days the *laibons* had dreams, and knew whether there is war or sickness or whether rain comes and where the herds should be driven." . . . But since the whites were in Africa, he said, no one had dreams any more. Dreams were no longer needed because the English knew everything![13]

Jung added that the *laibon* was "the living embodiment of the spreading disintegration of an undermined, outmoded, unrestorable world."[14]

Nevertheless, Jung records his experience of Africa as "one of the loveliest interludes in my life." He continues:

> I had the good fortune to taste the world of Africa, with its incredible beauty and its equally incredible suffering, before the end came. I enjoyed . . . "divine peace" . . . Never had I seen so clearly "man and other animals" (Herodotus). Thousands of miles lay between me and Europe, mother of all demons. The demons could not reach me here—there were no telegrams, no telephone calls, no letters, no visitors. My liberated psychic forces poured blissfully back to the primeval expanses.[15]

What a prophetic statement! Jung would have to deal with European demons, including some more of his own. Good and evil represent another pair of opposites that Jung would have to experience in depth and eventually transcend. In fact, underscoring this truth, one of the last things he wrote was on this essential topic: "Good and Evil in Analytical Psychology," which was completed in 1959, just two years before he died.

Union of Feminine and Masculine Within

In 1925, Jung published only one work: "Marriage as a Psychological Relationship," in which he focused on the evolution of marriage: "First it was passion, then it became duty, and finally an intolerable burden."[16] The key was to recognize that the "intolerable burden" was due to psychic disunity. Often in mid-life, there was a crisis having to do with one's outer marriage. In actuality, it concerned an "inner marriage" with the contrasexual aspect of the psyche, anima (feminine, soul) in a man and animus (masculine, spirit) in a woman. In other words, at the midpoint of life, one needed to love oneself and ideally then renew one's love with his or her spouse.

In the essay "Marriage as a Psychological Relationship," Jung says that he speaks from "personal experience" and that "one understands nothing psychological unless one has experienced it oneself."[17] Most likely Jung could say this at this time because he had left the entangled relationship with Sabina Spielrein, and he was struggling with his intimate relationship with Toni Wolff. He was developing insight, and his anima had some vision. However, Jung still had a long way to go! Fortunately for him, his "container" (a term he introduces in this essay), that is, his marriage to Emma, remained intact; and his wife stood by him through thick and thin. Foreshadowing Jung's involvement with *The Secret of the Golden Flower* was the intertwining of the primal pair of opposites: the female and male principles in his work.

Lao Tzu resonated with the truth of androgyny long ago. He says:

Whosoever knows his maleness . . .
guards his femaleness[18]

and

When male and female combine,
all things achieve harmony.[19]

In Chinese alchemy, and as noted in chapter 4, when water (yin) and fire (yang) are unified, the Golden Flower is born.[20] The Golden Flower manifests as "spirit" or "inner light" behind the eyes. It results from "circular motion" involving Taoist meditative exercises that cause the watery element from the kidneys to combine with the fire of the heart region representing inner intercourse of yin (female) and yang (male), yielding the birth of the Golden Flower.[21]

Chinese alchemy parallels European alchemy in postulating the change from watery lead (*negredo*) to fiery heart (*rebedo*) and then to pure white (*albedo*) or gold (also known as the Philosopher's Stone).[22]

Understandably, in ancient Greece, a "similar archetypal concept of a perfect being is that of Platonic man, round on all sides and uniting within himself the two sexes."[23]

The Secret of Richard Wilhelm

Jung first met Richard Wilhelm in 1922 at the School of Wisdom in Darmstadt, Germany. In 1923, Wilhelm brought out his German translation of *The I Ching or Book of Changes*, which Jung considered to be "the greatest of his achievements."[24] Jung had worked with Legge's inadequate rendering, so he "was therefore in a position to recognize fully the extraordinary difference between the two."[25]

But what was "the secret" that Wilhelm possessed? Jung recalled that in the place where they met—in a fertile "field of humanity"[26]—in the "point of contact; there leaped across a spark that kindled the light destined to become for me one of the most meaningful events of my life."[27] Jung viewed "Wilhelm and his work" as creating "a bridge between East and West."[28] Of course, Jung, through his collaboration with Wilhelm and others, helped make this bridge stronger and longer-lasting. Probably the most critical "inner marriage" that Jung would participate in was the inner union of East (introverted and feminine) and West (extraverted and masculine).

Jung maintained that Wilhelm "possessed in the highest degree the rare charisma of spiritual motherhood."[29] What did Wilhelm take in, contain, and give birth to? None other than "the Tao," which Wilhelm translated as "meaning."[30] So, Wilhelm's secret had to do with catalyzing Jung's acceptance of the Tao and meaning in his own life. He saw Wilhelm experiencing "Chinese wisdom as a living thing."[31] Jung viewed Wilhelm as "The messenger from China, . . . [who was] able to express profound things in plain language [which] disclose something of the simplicity of great truth and of deep meaning."[32]

What led Jung to say, "I feel myself so very much enriched by him that it seems to me as if I had received more from him than from any other man"?[33] He provided the answer right away: because Wilhelm "transplanted in the soil of the West a tender seedling, the Golden Flower, giving [Jung and] us a new intuition of life and meaning, as a relief from the tension of arbitrary will [ego] and arrogance [pride]."[34]

In 1927, Jung had created a most magnificent mandala that he called "Window on Eternity."[35] It was almost a prophetic prelude to what was to unfold (see plate 10). In 1928, Jung painted another mandala "with a golden castle in the center."[36] (See plate 11.) Jung asked himself, "Why is this so Chinese?"[37] As Jung recounts:

> I was impressed by the form and choice of colors, which seemed to me Chinese. . . . It was a strange coincidence that shortly afterward I received a letter from Richard Wilhelm enclosing the manuscript of a Taoist-alchemical treatise entitled *The Secret of the Golden Flower*, with a request that I write a commentary on it. I devoured the manuscript at once, for the text gave me undreamed-of confirmation of my ideas about the mandala and the circumambulation of the center. That was the first event which broke through my isolation. I became aware of an affinity; I could establish ties with something and someone.
>
> In remembrance of this coincidence, this "synchronicity," I wrote underneath the picture which had made so Chinese an impression upon me: "In 1928, when I was painting this picture, showing the golden, well-fortified castle, Richard Wilhelm in Frankfurt sent me the thousand-year-old Chinese text on the yellow castle, the germ of the immortal body."[38]

Writing the commentary on *The Secret of the Golden Flower: A Chinese Book of Life* served a healing function for Jung. He realized then—as he had from centering dreams and mandalas—"that the Self [was] the principle archetype of orientation and meaning. . . . Out of it emerged a first inkling of my personal myth."[39] When he wrote this as part of his commentary, it was as if Jung put an exclamation point after the last sentence:

> When I began my lifework in the practice of psychiatry and psychotherapy I was completely ignorant of the Chinese

PLATES 10 AND 11.
Two mandalas by Jung:
"Window on Eternity"

philosophy, and only later did my professional experience show me that in my technique I had been unconsciously led along that secret way which has been the preoccupation of the best minds of the East for centuries.[40]

Additionally, it was Wilhelm whom Jung saw as representing "the soul of Europe, who brings us new light from the East,"[41] and whom he called "that great interpreter of the soul of China"[42]—that illuminated Jung's own soul in his melan-

"The Golden Castle"

cholic but superbly creative work: *Modern Man in Search of a Soul*.[43]

The Candle Dims

Despite the 1929 publication and promise of *The Secret of the Golden Flower*, icy and at times gale-force winds blew in from the north. The flame of the soul died down and during the 1930s it nearly went out. As Jung says:

Every good quality has its bad side, and nothing good can come into the world without at once producing a corresponding evil.[44]

As mentioned before, Lao Tzu had a similar view:

The Tao doesn't take sides;
it gives birth to both good and evil.[45]

During the early 1930s, Jung was productive. He wrote on fundamental areas of his psychology: "The Stages of Life" (1930), "Some Aspects of Modern Psychotherapy" (1930), "Basic Postulates of Analytical Psychology" (1931), and "Aims of Psychotherapy" (1931). Jung extended his psychology to include literature and art: "Psychology and Literature" (1930), "Ulysses" (1932), and "Picasso" (1932). The last work on Picasso seems a bit odd. Jung appears to get into the persona role of psychiatrist and in an ego-dominated way makes the judgment that Picasso must be a schizophrenic. This is a strange essay, since there are certain similarities between Picasso's and Jung's troubled relationships with women (thus, mother and anima problems), but, most important, they are both profoundly creative individuals. Actually, Jung was also a very talented artist, which he denied. Therefore, could this condemnation of Picasso be a projection? This issue is raised here because at about the same time, Jung was already displaying denial—one of the two most primitive defense mechanisms, the other being projection—in his reaction to the pleas of two Jewish colleagues about the rise of Nazism.

The Jewish Question

In 1933, Jung turned his back on the path of the Tao and took a dangerous detour that associated him with Nazi Germany.

As Lao Tzu says:

The Great Way is easy,
Yet people prefer the side paths,
Be aware when things are out of balance.[46]

Unfortunately, Jung was not aware that he was caught in a shadow complex involving his German Fatherland—a nation with delusions of grandeur led by a madman. Furthermore, Jung was unaware of another maxim of Lao Tzu's: "Success is as dangerous as failure,"[47] and he lapsed back into political power persona roles fueled by shadow energy. Jung became president of the German-based General Medical Society for Psychotherapy, the founding president of the International General Medical Society of Psychotherapy, and an editor of *Zentralblatt für Psychotherapie und ihre Grenzgebiete.* All this was similar to the persona roles and ego-inflated positions he had held in the Freudian international movement, which also included a key editorial task. The problem was the anti-Semitic position of the Nazis; these medical organizations and the journal interfaced with or were influenced—knowingly or unknowingly—by Nazi propaganda.

Lao Tzu's comment is pertinent to the coming catastrophe:

The reason I experience great evil is that I have a persona.[48]

To illustrate how far Jung had strayed off the Taoist path, let me share the stories of two devout Jews who ought to have been able to convince an open, sensitive, receptive Jung of the true nature of the Nazi scourge. Either of two religious Jews (Erich Neumann and James Kirsch), who were very close to Jung, could have served the function of *Rebbe* for Jung.[49] *Rebbe* is a term used by Rabbi Levi Meier[50] for his Jungian analyst, James Kirsch. The rabbi considered James Kirsch to be his *Rebbe* (like a rabbi, but more of a personal spiritual guide or mentor). When Jung's dear friend and colleague Erich Neumann attempted to play the *Rebbe* role for Jung, he was ignored. Jung's "blind spot," or shadow problem, became a "hearing spot," or psychological deafness. Before he left Zürich for Palestine, Neumann pleaded with Jung to wake up to the dangers of Nazi Germany.

Years later Neumann's son, Micha, reported:

> My father told me he tried to convince Jung of the terrible danger of the Nazi movement, of the brutality and inhumanity of the Nazis. He asked Jung to express himself openly and clearly against their ideologies and especially their anti-Semitic ideas and policies. He admitted that he failed to change Jung's attitude. My father warned him that if he kept quiet at such a bad time for the Jews, then it would always be remembered and he would never be forgiven. Jung, believing in the qualities of the German collective unconscious, insisted that something positive might emerge from the situation.[51]

This is an example of Jung not listening to Erich Neumann, and it persisted after Neumann got to Palestine. In fact, until he had his heart attack in 1944, Jung remained unable to take in the meaning (and soul) of Judaism.[52]

Since James Kirsch had lived in Berlin, and knew Jung well from 1929 to 1961, he, too, ought to have been able to serve in a *Rebbe* capacity for Jung. Echoing Neumann's warnings to Jung, Kirsch maintained that Jung simply did not believe him when he told him about the Nazi terror directed against the Jews.[53] However, Jung, as characteristic of his own psychology and of the individuation process itself, had to find his own way to the truth.

Jung was unable to adhere to his own insightful words, written in 1933 and 1934:

> The political and social isms of our day preach every conceivable ideal, but, under this mask, they pursue the goal of lowering the level of our culture by restricting or altogether

inhibiting the possibilities of individual development. They do this partly by creating a chaos controlled by terrorism, a primitive state of affairs that affords only the barest necessities of life and surpasses in horror the worst times of the so-called "Dark" Ages. It remains to be seen whether this experience of degradation and slavery will once more raise a cry for greater spiritual freedom.[54]

From 1933 to 1939, Jung seemed gripped by a power complex and caught in a trancelike state by his shadow.[55] He exhibited a strange but human dependence on power and shadow.

Chuang Tzu had long ago written words that now expressed Jung's predicament:

My dependence is like that of the snake on his skin. How can I tell why I do this, or why I do that?[56]

This statement makes reference to the serpent, symbol of healing and the death/rebirth process—something that awaits Jung anew, but unfortunately it is a decade away.

Again, Jung fell into darkness. Aniela Jaffé, Jung's trusted friend, colleague, and confidante, who recorded and edited *Memories, Dreams, Reflections*, was herself a Jew, and said in response to rumors that were rampant during the Nazi regime, especially during 1933 to 1935, "Jung was neither a Nazi nor an anti-Semite."[57] She ought to have known, since she knew him better than did most people. Jung actually helped her after she was able to get out of Nazi Germany. Nevertheless, Jaffé also said, "Criticism of Jung's attitude during 1933 and 1934 is justified by the facts."[58] For example, Jaffé attributed the following statement to Jung's shadow side:[59]

The Jew, who is something of a nomad, has never yet created a cultural form of his own . . . since all his instincts and talents require a more or less civilized nation to act as a host for their development.[60]

Jung also discussed the difference between "Jewish" and "German" psychologies.[61] Fortunately, in due course, Jung saw this for what it was: senseless. During Siegmund Hurwitz's analysis with Jung (after World War II), Hurwitz (a deeply committed Jew) told him about how troubled he was by some of Jung's earlier writings, such as the 1934 article entitled "The State of Psychotherapy Today." Replying to Hurwitz, Jung said that he now considered that article to be "nonsense."[62]

Jaffé does provide a brief windless moment for Jung's soul to rekindle, in as much as she notes:

> When Jung spoke of the difference of Jewish psychology he did not, like the Nazi, imply "depreciation" of it. Jung saw the Jews as "a race with a three-thousand-year-old civilization" and he saw the Germanic "Aryans" as exhibiting a "youthfulness not yet fully weaned from barbarism."[63]

It is significant that the above comment contradicts his previous statement about the Jews as nomads with no autonomous culture of their own. What we can conclude is that Jung was inconsistent, neurotic, and out of balance in a Taoist sense. Jaffé summed it up when she said he made a "grave human error."[64] I think Barbara Hannah's 1934 pencil sketch of Jung captures the essence of a very troubled man (see plate 12). Remember "Ka," who followed Philemon and Elijah in the vision after the fall into darkness subsequent to the break with Freud? Recall that Ka's expression was "demonic [and] Mephistophelian."[65] I think Ka was the source of the problematic statements and actions by Jung during the Nazi period. Jung viewed Ka as a trickster demon, like Mercurius.

It is my supposition that Jung was dependent on the "wisdom of speech" (of words). However, as Thomas Merton once elo-

PLATE 12.
Portrait of Jung, 1934, by Barbara Hannah

quently stated, "To attain . . . spiritual wisdom, one must first be liberated from servile dependence on the 'wisdom of speech' (1. Cor. 1:17)."[66] Jung needed badly the wisdom of the serpent and his proverbial stone—the spiritual healing of the East. Nevertheless, it would be years before Jung got off his potentially destructive detour and back on the Way of integrity. A guiding metaphorical image for Jung to strive to attain could have been the Zen maxim: "One mirror reflecting another with no shadow between them."[67]

In contrast to Ka, Philemon was seen as the "spiritual aspect, or 'meaning.'"[68] Jung notes, "In time I was able to integrate both figures through the study of alchemy."[69] Jung made attempts to integrate his split in the 1935 and 1936 Eranos papers on alchemy (published in 1944 as *Psychology and Alchemy*), but wasn't successful until the 1955 publication of his magnum opus, *Mysterium Coniunctionis*.

James Kirsch provides commentary that this actually transpired:

> I could see that [Jung] had grown out of that frame of mind [and the Ka-based anti-Semitic statements], and . . . I knew to what great extent he had become conscious of his own Jewish psychology . . . [see *Answer to Job* and *Mysterium Coniunctionis*, paragraphs 591–95 (pp. 410–15) and 619 (429–31)]. He [also] shows a deep understanding of the psychological causes of anti-Semitism [*Mysterium Coniunctionis*, paragraph 646 (p. 330)].[70]

Erich Neumann had a similar view of Jung's *Answer to Job*, as revealed in letters that also show Jung was very conscious of his own individuation process. On December 5, 1951, Neumann wrote to Jung about his not-yet-published *Answer to Job*:

> This is a book that conquered me to my depth. I think it is the most beautiful and deepest of your writings . . . it is a dialogue and dispute with God, similar to that of Abraham, when he argued with God about the fate of Sodom. For me personally it is like an accusation sheet against God, who allowed six million of his people to be killed.[71]

Jung's reply to Neumann's letter came soon, on January 5, 1952: "I thank you very much for your friendly letter and the way you understand me. This compensates for a thousand misunderstandings."[72]

Jung maintained that he embodied both "*Faust*, the inept, pur-blind philosopher, [and] . . . [Faust's] dark side of his being, his sinister shadow, *Mephistopheles.*"73 Jung stated this energetically: "The dichotomy of Faust-Mephistopheles came together within myself into a single person, and I was that person."74

At Bollingen, Jung's self (his personal being) was ideally in touch with the Self through his inner Taoist master Philemon. In fact, over the gate of the original Tower, Jung inscribed "Shrine of Philemon—Repentance of Faust."75

Experiencing "Death" and the Coming "Rebirth"

In 1935, at the age of sixty, Jung signaled a return to his Eastern path by writing a psychological commentary on *The Tibetan Book of the Dead.*76 My supposition is that he used this book of instructions for the dead and dying to prepare himself for the demise of his "Ka" shadow part (or negative ego-identity). Jung apparently had been working on this "death" a long time, as he states, "For years, ever since it was first published, the *Bardo Thödol* [Tibetan title for *The Tibetan Book of the Dead*], has been my constant companion."77 This illuminating work concerns life after death and a subsequent initiatory rebirth (reincarnation in the womb). Jung is quick to point out that

> the only [such death and rebirth] "initiation process" that is still alive and practiced today in the West is the analysis of the unconscious as used by doctors for therapeutic purposes.78

My further assumption is that here, too, the seeds are being sown for Jung's additional future shamanistic self-healing experiences.

It was also in 1935 that Jung added a fourth part to Bollingen (see plate 13). As he states:

PLATE 13.
The Loggia from above

The desire arose in me for a piece of fenced-in land. I needed a larger space that would stand open to the sky and to nature. And so . . . I added a courtyard and a loggia by the lake, which formed a fourth element that was separated from the unitary threeness [masculinity] of the house. Thus a quaternity [feminity] had arisen, four different parts of the building, and, moreover, in the course of twelve years.79

During the following year, in 1936, Jung worked on "Religious Ideas in Alchemy" (later published as part III of *Psychology and Alchemy*. He also wrote about the anima concept,[80] as the healing nature of the feminine soul, which is something that Jung clearly needed at this point in his life.

In 1937, by being selected to give the Terry lectures at Yale University on "Psychology and Religion,"[81] Jung was bestowed a great honor that seems to have also served as a transcendent function.[82] As a transitional objective experience, this exercise appears to have catalyzed the renewal process of unification for Jung that would not come to fruition until 1957, when he wrote *The Undiscovered Self (Present and Future)*.[83] In this book, published when he was eighty-two, Jung shares how to become conscious enough to create objective meaning in our lives and take full responsibility for ourselves, our fate, and even the fate of our world.[84]

In 1938, in "Psychological Aspects of the Mother Archetype,"[85] Jung continued to pursue the feminine theme. Most significantly, in this same year, Jung visited India, the land of the collective mother. All of this suggests that Jung was mothering (loving and nurturing) himself more and more in his psychic womb, preparing for rebirth, which he wrote about next.[86]

As Jung says in his autobiography, "India affected me like a dream, for I was and remained in search of myself, of the truth peculiar to myself."[87]

At this time, Jung was so engrossed in the study of alchemy that he took the first volume of the *Theatrum Chemicum* (1602) along with him to India. It contains the primary writings of Gerardus Dorneus, which would later be central to the writing of *Mysterium Coniunctionis*.

Alchemy was helpful to Jung in facing the dark shadow and paralleling that experience: "In India [he] was principally concerned with the question of the psychological nature of evil."[88]

Jung was intrigued "by the way this problem [of evil] is integrated in Indian spiritual life, and [he] saw it in a new light."[89] Jung continued to reflect on his experience:

The Indian's goal is not moral perfection, but the condition of *nirdvandva*. He wishes to free himself from nature; in keeping with this aim, he seeks in meditation the condition of imagelessness and emptiness. I, on the other hand, wish to persist in the state of lively contemplation of nature and of the psychic images. I want to be freed neither from human beings, nor from myself, nor from nature; for all these appear to me the greatest of miracles. Nature, the psyche, and life appear to me like divinity unfolded—and what more could I wish for? To me the supreme meaning of Being can consist only in the fact that it *is*, not that it is not or is no longer.[90]

Jung adds (as if a prelude to his coming psychological commentary to *The Tibetan Book of the Great Liberation*):

To me there is no liberation *à tout prix*. I cannot be liberated from anything that I do not possess, have not done or experienced. Real liberation becomes possible for me only when I have done all that I was able to do, when I have completely devoted myself to a thing and participated in it to the utmost. If I withdraw from participation, I am virtually amputating the corresponding part of my psyche. Naturally, there may be good reasons for my not immersing myself in a given experience. But then I am forced to confess my inability, and must know that I may have neglected to do something of vital importance. In this way I make amends for the lack of a positive act by the clear knowledge of my incompetence.[91]

And lastly Jung states (almost prophetically):

A man who has not passed through the inferno of his passions has never overcome them. . . . Whenever we give up, leave behind, and forget too much, there is always the danger that the things we have neglected will return with added force.92

One of the most moving experiences of Jung's in India involved the Buddha. Jung says:

When I visited the stupas of Sanchi, where Buddha delivered his fire sermon, I was overcome by a strong emotion of the kind that frequently develops in me when I encounter a thing, person, or idea, of whose significance I am still unconscious. . . . The stupas are tombs or containers of relics, hemispherical in shape, like two gigantic rice bowls placed one on top of the other (concavity upon concavity), according to the prescripts of the Buddha himself in the *Mahâ-Parinibbâna-Sutta.* [The path] leads into a clockwise circumambulation around the stupa[s]. . . . The distant prospect over the plain, the stupas themselves, the temple ruins, and the solitary stillness of this holy site held me in a spell. . . . A new side of Buddhism was revealed to me there. I grasped the life of the Buddha as the reality of the self which had broken through and laid claim to a personal life . . . Buddha saw and grasped the cosmogonic dignity of human consciousness; for that reason he saw clearly that if a man succeeded in extinguishing this light, the world would sink into nothingness.93

Zen is "a product of the meeting of speculative Indian Buddhism with practical Chinese Taoism and even Confucianism."94

The essence of Zen is that there is nothing beyond what is. Perhaps why Jung liked Buddhism was its insistence on "personal experience"[95] as its foundation, much like Jung's analytical psychology. Both help the individual become independent of his or her persona and dominated ego.[96] What Zen calls the "Great Death" leads to a state of "no self," or what Thomas Merton and Jung call the "true self."[97]

Both Merton[98] and Jung[99] wrote about D. T. Suzuki and his work. Merton equates Suzuki with such universally known figures as Einstein and Gandhi,[100] adding that Suzuki embodies "all the indefinable qualities of the 'Superior Man' of the ancient Asian Taoist, Confucian, and Buddhist traditions."[101]

Jung also lauds Suzuki:

> [His] works on Zen Buddhism are among the best contributions to the knowledge of living Buddhism that recent decades have produced, and Zen itself is the most important fruit to have sprung from the tree whose roots are the collection of the Pali Canon. We cannot be sufficiently grateful to [Suzuki], first for having brought Zen closer to Western understanding, and secondly for the manner in which he has performed this task.[102]

In his foreword to Suzuki's *Introduction to Zen Buddhism*, Jung let the statements of Zen masters that Suzuki writes about testify as to what "enlightenment," or *satori,* the goal of Zen, is truly about. For example:

> A monk once went to Gensha, and wanted to learn where the entrance to the path of truth was. Gensha answered him, "Do you hear the murmuring of the brook?" "Yes, I hear it," answered the monk. "There is the entrance," the Master instructed him.[103]

Jung notes that the origin of Zen seems to be Buddha's Flower Sermon. As Jung says, "On this occasion [Buddha] held up a flower to a gathering of disciples without uttering a word."[104]

Recall again Lao Tzu's wise words:

He who knows does not speak,
He who speaks does not know.[105]

In reviewing Suzuki's work, Jung says that Zen is "an experience of transformation. . . . It is not that something is seen, but that one sees differently."[106] Jung sees:

Great as is the value of Zen Buddhism for understanding the religious transformation process, its use among Western people is very problematical.[107]

Jung assesses "the goal" of Zen and analytical psychology as the same: "Transformation," based on "the disappearance of ego-hood."[108] However, he warns that the Westerner lacks the cultural basis and context for Zen. Furthermore, he cautions the unaware person who pursues Zen of "unknown terrors and dangers . . . [especially] the worst of all fates threatens the venturer: mute, abysmal loneliness."[109]

Jung favors psychotherapy over Buddhism, ideally in-depth therapy based on analytical psychology. "The attainment of wholeness requires one to stake one's whole being. Nothing less will do; there can be no easier conditions, no substitutes, no compromises."[110] Furthermore, he admonishes us: "If you have nothing at all to create, then perhaps you create yourself."[111] However, Jung seems too cautious regarding Zen Buddhism, because both Mokusen Miyuki[112] and Kitaro Nishida[113] outline the same individuation process toward wholeness using Zen that Jung does emphasizing "self-realization" and "a 'true self'–'Absolute Self' axis."[114]

Nevertheless, very late in his life, Jung is clear about Buddha's wisdom having helped him immensely.[115]

Heart and Soul Attack

Harkening back to Mountain Lake's words—a score of years before Jung's heart attack—regarding the white man's need to think with his heart, not his head, listen to *The Secret of the Golden Flower:*

> At the time of birth the conscious spirit inhales the energy and thus becomes the dwelling of the new-born. It lives in the heart. From that time on the heart is master, and the primal spirit loses its place while the conscious spirit [the head] has the power.
>
> The primal spirit loves stillness, and the conscious spirit loves movement.
>
> . . . If the spirit-energy is turbid and unclean, it crystallizes downward, sinks down to hell, and becomes a demon.
>
> If one wants to maintain the primal spirit one must, without fail, first subjugate the perceiving spirit. The way to subjugate it is through the circulation of the light. If one practices the circulation of the light, one must forget both body and heart. The heart must die, the spirit live.[116]

> The awakening of the spirit is accomplished because the heart has first died. When a man can let his heart die, then the primal spirit wakes to life. To kill the heart does not mean to let it dry and wither away, but it means that it has become undivided and gathered into one.
>
> The Buddha said, "When you fix your heart on one point, then nothing is impossible for you."[117]

As Jung had experienced once before, when he broke from Freud and his ego-image and identity had to die, "darkness gives birth to light."[118]

Jung was to once more fall into the abyss of darkness. His heart and soul would be attacked, and he would become deathly ill. This near-death experience would be transforming, as Jung himself wrote in his "Commentary" to *The Secret of the Golden Flower*: "The Gods have become diseases."[119] Now, he would experience that in a Buddhist and Taoist fashion firsthand!

At this point, we can add to Jung's statement above, "the East has taught us ... more profound, and higher understanding through life—[and near-death]."[120] Out of his near-fatal heart attack he realized that "the empty chamber grows light."[121]

Jung was destined to travel to

the center of emptiness ... [the Taoists'] ancestral land, or the yellow castle, or the dark pass, or the space of former heaven. The heavenly heart is like the dwelling place, the light is the master.[122]

How do we outgrow our problems? Jung prophetically answers this question himself, when he recommends "*wu wei* (action through non-action) [i.e., and] let things happen."[123]

Let us recall Jung's mandala of 1928, "the golden castle," which was related to his synchronous receipt of *The Secret of the Golden Flower* manuscript from Richard Wilhelm.

As prologue to Jung's experience,

The origin of the great Way (the Tao) [is] the heavenly heart. . . . . If you can be absolutely quiet then the heavenly heart will spontaneously manifest itself.[124]

When the body heart dies (is attacked) then the light of the primal spirit can enter. Furthermore, the earth-water body, yin (dark, dead, empty, receptive heart), must mate with the heavenly spirit-fire, yang, for the Golden Flower to be created. These Taoist experiences awaited Jung.

The key transcendent function for Jung's alchemy was his heart. My conjecture is that Jung's "heart attack" in 1944, which occurred after a fall, was also a "soul/spirit attack" based on the realization that he'd been wrong about the German psyche (and his own).[125] It was only a year later that he wrote, "After the Catastrophe."[126] In this piece, Jung comes very close to making a confession about being mistaken regarding the Nazis. He does refer to "stopping [up his] ears," which would relate to his inability to hear the warnings of his Jewish colleagues and friends. Jung sums it up when he says:

> While I was working on this article I noticed how churned up one still is in one's own psyche, and how difficult it is to reach anything approaching a moderate and relatively calm point of view in the midst of one's emotions. No doubt we should be cold-blooded and superior; but we are, on the whole, much more deeply involved in the recent events in Germany than we like to admit. . . . I must confess that no article has ever given me so much trouble, from a moral as well as a human point of view. I had not realized how much I myself was affected. . . . This inner identity or *participation mystique* with events in Germany has caused me to experience afresh how painfully wide is the scope of the psychological concept of *collective guilt*. So when I approach this problem it is certainly not with any feelings of cold-blooded superiority, but rather with an avowed sense of inferiority.[127]

The visions that Jung had during his heart attack are so meaningful that they are worth reviewing. Jung thought his nurse in the hospital was "an old Jewish woman [who] was preparing ritual kosher dishes for [him]." Jung confided, "When I looked at her, she seemed to have a blue halo around her head."[128] The most telling scene of all followed when Jung saw himself in the Pardes Rimmonim (the garden of pomegranates)[129] and the wedding of Tifereth and Malchuth was taking place. Then Jung stated an archetypal truth:

> Or else I was the Rabbi Simon ben Jochai, whose wedding in the afterlife was being celebrated. It was the mystic marriage as it appears in the Cabbalistic tradition. . . . At bottom it was I myself: I was the marriage. And my beatitude was that of a blissful wedding.[130]

Jung reflected on this memory, which seems to have been a moment of epiphany:

> There is something else I quite distinctly remember. At the beginning, when I was having the vision of the garden of pomegranates, I asked the nurse to forgive me if she were harmed. . . . There was a *pneuma* of inexpressible sanctity in the room, whose manifestation was the *mysterium coniunctionis*.[131]

In this individuating attack on Jung's own heart and primal spirit, Jung found that "to experience defeat is also to experience victory."[132] The victory Jung claimed was rebirth of his heart and spirit. Jung now saw the world differently. As Barbara Hannah records:

> There was also a vision or experience—not mentioned in *Memories*—which he described to Emma Jung and myself very vividly. . . . he felt that his body had been dismembered and cut up into small pieces. Then, over quite a long period,

it was slowly collected and put together again with the greatest care. This is a very interesting parallel to the widespread primitive rituals that were experienced by shamans. [Jung said] that he had been obliged to do most of or all of the reassembling himself.[133]

This is an example par excellence of the "wounded healer" archetype in operation, so to speak.

As we know, Jung favored water (anima/feminine) over fire (animus/masculine), but both are necessary for a creative, whole life. "*Fire* is spirit, *water* is vitality. Alchemists sometimes say that Buddhism starts with *fire* while Taoism starts with *water*."[134]

Jung's victory involves replacing "false yin" (yin inside fire) with "true yin" (calmness). "The operation referred to as 'taking from *water* to fill in *fire*' consists of replacing [the false yin] (temporal [ego] conditioning) inside *fire* (consciousness [ego]) with the ['true yang'] (real knowledge) inside *water* (the depths of the unconscious)."[135] "This formula," according to Thomas Cleary, "comes from the alchemical classic *Understanding Reality*, by Liu I-ming, which says, "Take the solid in the heart of the position of *water,* and change the yin in the innards of the palace of *fire*. From this transformation comes the sound body of heaven [and renewal heart] (the creative)."[136]

In 1946, Jung suffered a second heart attack, which he felt was due to the fact that he had still not solved

the mysterious problem of the *hieros gamos* (the *mysterium coniunctionis*) . . . [Jung] again found himself confronted, like medicine men all over the world, with curing himself.[137]

In the next, and last, chapter we will see how Jung continues to heal himself. Proceeding with his individuation and self-actualization process, Jung could now spend the rest of his reborn life answering the following questions posed by his spirit/soul mate Lao Tzu:

Can you educate your soul so that
  it encompasses the One
  without dispersing itself?
Can you make your strength unitary
  and achieve that softness
  that makes you like a little child?
Can you cleanse your secret seeing
  so that it becomes free of stain?
Can you love [others] and rule [the Institute]
  so that you remain without knowledge?
Can you, when the gates of Heaven
  open and close, be like the female bird?
Can you penetrate everything with your inner
  clarity and purity
  without having need for action?
Generating and nourishing,
generating and not possessing,
being effective and not retaining,
increasing and not dominating:
this is the secret [of] Life [and of Integrity].[138]

Chapter 6

Sunset and Return to the Self:

*Resolution of Jung's
Late-Life Crisis*

The Way . . . can be used to withdraw for self-cultivation. [1]

LAO TZU

*What is meant by the Self is not only in me but in all beings, like the
. . . Tao. It is psychic totality.* [2]

CARL JUNG

In 1947, when he was seventy-two years old, Jung retired to
Bollingen. The word "retired" means to have withdrawn or gone
to a private, sheltered, or secluded place. [3] This definition fits ex-
actly with Jung's move to Bollingen and with the third part of the
opportunity character that represents this final part of the hexagram of Jung's life. Here, Jung as an individual, on his way to
self-actualization, guards the frontier to consciousness and enlight-

enment, which again is very similar to, if not the same as, his withdrawal to his *Temenos* (sacred space) at Bollingen. The second definition for "retired" is that a person "has gone to bed." And stories are told at bedtime all over the world. Jung once said, "The crucial thing is the story. For it alone shows the human background and the human suffering."[4] A conversation between Jung and his good friend Laurens van der Post reflects this philosophy (van der Post had just returned from the Kalahari Desert and was telling Jung how distressed he was that the Bushman culture had been destroyed because their stories had been taken away by the whites):

> [Jung] nodded his fine white head as the wind released a far-off refrain among the leaves of the trees he had planted as a young man at Bollingen, because they were living and viable thoughts of God to him. He went on, in that deep bass voice of his, to tell me, at great length, how his work as a healer did not take wing . . . until he realized that the key to the human personality was its story. Every human being at core, he held, had a unique story and no man could discover his greatest meaning unless he lived and, as it were, grew his own story.[5]

Jung had grown his own story. Or, more accurately, it had unfolded and materialized in stone at Bollingen. Ever since he had had his mandalic Liverpool dream in 1927, Jung never again sank into despair. As Barbara Hannah stated, "He knew there was a light at the center of every individual life, . . . where the opposites are harmoniously united . . . at the center."[6] This dream, which Jung called an "act of grace," provided him with his first vivid image of the nature of the Self.[7]

As Jung says about this "turning point" dream,

> Everything round about was obscured by rain, fog, smoke, and dimly lit darkness, the little island blazed with sunlight.

On it stood a single tree, a magnolia, in a shower of reddish blossoms.[8]

Carried away by the beauty of the flowering tree and the sunlit island, he thought, "I know very well why he has settled [in Liverpool]. Then I awoke."[9] Jung reflected:

This dream represented my situation at the time. . . .[10] Everything was extremely unpleasant, black . . . just as I felt then. But I had had a vision of unearthly beauty, and that was why I was able to live at all, Liverpool is the "pool of life." The "liver," according to an old view, is the seat of life . . . that which "makes to live."

This dream brought with it a sense of finality. I saw that here the goal had been revealed. One could not go beyond the center. The center is the goal, and everything is directed toward that center. Through this dream I understood that the Self is the principle and archetype of orientation and meaning [hence, the Tao according to Richard Wilhelm[11]]. Therein lies its healing function. For me, this insight signified an approach to the center and therefore to the goal. Out of it emerged a first inkling of my personal myth.[12]

What Jung had accomplished through his "creative illness," his "confrontation with the unconscious," was to begin healing himself by growing his own story or personal myth; that is, to allow his tree of life to grow, develop, flower, and bear fruit. In the last phase of Jung's life at Bollingen, he was able to reap from his life-tree the benefits of what he had sown during his first seven decades. We, too, have benefited from Jung's sunset years, when he integrated yin and yang forces and became a modest person in harmony with Nature. Out of this humble, and at times rather childlike, state, Jung created some of his most profound works.

Barbara Hannah wrote, "I have never seen anyone else attain the simplicity which was the essence of Jung."[13] What Hannah had seen was the Taoist sage in Jung who embodied Lao Tzu's admonition, "Embrace the simplicity of the unhewn log."[14]

In ancient China, Lao Tzu could be describing Jung:

Whoever knows his honor
and guards his shame:
he is the valley of the world.
If he is the valley of the world
he finds satisfaction in eternal Life
and returns to simplicity.[15]

Finally, broadening the concept of simplicity to show its rootedness in the Tao and how this leads to peace, Lao Tzu says:

The Tao never does anything,
yet through it all things are done.

If powerful men and women
could center themselves in it,
the whole world would be transformed
by itself, in its natural rhythms.
People would be content
with their simple, everyday lives,
in harmony, and free of desire.

When there is no desire,
all things are at peace.[16]

Jung reflects on being at his retreat:

At Bollingen I am in the midst of my true life, I am most deeply myself. Here I am, as it were, the "age-old son of the mother." That is how alchemy puts it, very wisely, for the "old man", the "ancient", whom I thought I had already experienced as a child, is personality No. 2, who has always been and always will be. He exists outside time and is the son of the maternal unconscious. In my fantasies he took the form of Philemon [Jung's Taoist Master], and he comes to life again at Bollingen.[17]

Lao Tzu, the original Taoist, says:

"Existence" I call the mother of individual beings.[18]

I am different from ordinary people.
I drink from the Great Mother's breasts.[19]

There was something formless and perfect
before the universe was born.
It is serene. Empty.
Infinite. Eternally present.
It is the mother of the universe.
For lack of a better name,
I call it the Tao.[20]

Chuang Tzu's words also interrelate the sacred place of Bollingen and its alchemical source—the maternal unconscious:

The spirit has an impregnable Tower
which no danger can disturb
As long as the tower is guarded
By the invisible Protector
Who acts unconsciously.[21]

Living at Bollingen, Jung was at one with Mother Nature. As he says:

At times I feel as if I am spread out over the landscape and inside things, and am myself living in every tree, in the splashing of the waves, in the clouds and the animals that come and go, in the procession of the seasons. There is nothing in the Tower that has not grown into its own form over the decades, nothing with which I am not linked. Here everything has its history, and mine; here is space for the spaceless kingdom of the world's and the psyche's hinterland.

PLATE 14.
Jung chopping wood at Bollingen

I have done without electricity, and tend the fireplace
and stove myself. Evenings, I light the old lamps. There is
no running water, and I pump water from the well. I chop
the wood [see plate 14] and cook the food. These simple
acts make man simple; and how difficult it is to be simple![22]

Jung continues:

In Bollingen, silence surrounds me almost audibly, and I
live "in modest harmony with nature."[23] Thoughts rise to
the surface which reach back into the centuries, and accord-
ingly anticipate a remote future. Here the torment of creation is lessened; creativity and play are close together.[24]

Child's Play and Creativity

As we all know, a small child is often simple, unconscious, and
partakes freely in the mysterious world of Mother Nature. We say
"That's child's play," but most of us secretly want to play as well.
One of Jung's great gifts to himself specifically and to the healing
process in general was to underscore the value of child's play,
which embodies the realm of the symbol and active imagination.

Apropos is something recorded by Chuang Tzu, but said by
Lin Hui:

My bond with the child
Was the bond of Tao.[25]

We know that as a child, Jung liked to play; but his play was
often lonely. For example, we explored his early intimate relationship with the stone, when he was seven to nine. Later, during
very stressful times, Jung returned to his boyhood friend, the
stone, for solace and healing.

As a nine- or ten-year-old, Jung had a passion for building

"little houses and castles, using bottles to form sides of gates and vaults . . . [and] ordinary stones, with mud for mortar."[26] After the painful break with Freud, while in a state of despair, Jung discovered again his inner child. As he put it, "The small boy is still around, and possesses a creative life which I lack."[27]

However, Jung wondered, "How can I make my way to it?"[28] Then he pondered:

> For as a grown man it seemed impossible to me that I should be able to bridge the distance from the present back to [age ten]. Yet I wanted to re-establish contact with that period, I had no choice but to return to it and take up once more that child's life. . . . This moment was a turning point in my fate, but I gave in only after endless resistances and with a sense of resignation. For it was a painfully humiliating experience to realize there was nothing to be done except play. . . .
>
> I began accumulating suitable stones. . . . And I started

PLATE 15.
Bear rolling a ball and woman milking a mare
(The original outer Tower wall)

building: cottages, a castle, a whole village [including a church with an altar]. . . .

I went on with my building game after the noon meal everyday, whenever the weather permitted. As soon as I was through eating, I began playing, and continued to do so until the patients arrived; and if I was finished with my work early enough in the evening, I went back to building. In the course of this activity my thoughts clarified, and I was able to grasp the fantasies whose presence in myself I dimly felt.[29]

What Jung had found was the vital connection between the child within, play, active imagination, creativity, and healing. No

PLATE 16.
A bull and more (Relief on the inner wall of the Loggia)

small feat, it was healing for Jung and for many others who have pursued the same path.[30] As Jung said, "This sort of thing has been consistent with me, and at any time in my life when I came up against a blank wall, I painted a picture or hewed a stone."[31] Bollingen holds ample evidence of this with Jung's sculptures, paintings, stone carvings, and (of course) Bollingen itself (see plates 15 and 16). When I visited this special place, Peter Jung showed me where his grandfather used to engage in "water works" (see plate 17).[32] Beaming with memories, Peter told me of wonderful experiences of helping his grandfather build dams, canals, tunnels, and bridges where the stream comes down from the hills into the lake. It was pure child's play, and it would eventually wash away like sand castles on the beach, but at the lakeshore it would take much longer for it to melt into the water.

PLATE 17.
Grandfather Jung playing creatively with his grandchildren.

Ting/The Cauldron
No. 50

Chin/Progress
No. 35

FIGURE 6.1.

Jung's First *I Ching* Hexagrams

theories. . . . It is of course disquieting, and one is not certain whether the compass is pointing true or not; but security, certitude, and peace do not lead to discoveries. . . .

It is by no means easy to feel one's way into such a remote and mysterious mentality as that underlying the *I Ching*. One cannot easily disregard such great minds as Confucius and Lao Tzu, [nor] . . . can one overlook the fact that the *I Ching* was their main source of inspiration. I know that previously I would not have dared to express myself so explicitly about so uncertain a matter. I can take this risk because I am now in my eighth decade, and the changing opinions of [people] scarcely impress me anymore; the thoughts of the old masters are of greater value to me than the philosophical prejudices of the Western mind.43

Jung then boldly asks the *I Ching* what it thinks about his action to write the foreword in the first place. The answer was hexagram 29, *K'an,* the Abysmal. But the third line is a changing line—because it is a six (all three coins were heads), it changes from a yin line into its opposite, yang, which is nine (see figure 6.2).

K'an or the Abysmal indicates a "downward" direction and

means "a pit."[44] While there are clear dangers, this hexagram also comforted Jung with this statement: "If you are sincere, you have success in your heart."[45] The changing line converts this hexagram to *Ching,* or the Well (see figure 6.2). Jung's second hexagram, *Ching*/Well, indicates "union" and it nourishes like the Caldron (*Ting,* 50): "The well brings about discrimination as to what is right."[46]

As Jung concludes his foreward to the *I Ching,* still treating the book as if it were an individual who was an oracle, he states:

> In view of the *I Ching*'s extreme age and its Chinese origin, I cannot consider its archaic, symbolic, and flowery language abnormal. On the contrary, I . . . congratulate this hypothetical person on the extent of his insight into my unexpressed state of doubt.[47]

Finally, Jung says:

> The *I Ching* does not offer itself with proofs and results; it does not vaunt itself, nor is it easy to approach. Like a part of nature, it waits until it is discovered. It offers neither facts nor power, but for lovers of self-knowledge, of wisdom—if there be such—it seems to be the right book. . . . Let it go

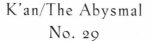

K'an/The Abysmal
No. 29

Ching/The Well
No. 48

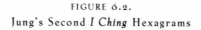

FIGURE 6.2.
Jung's Second *I Ching* Hexagrams

forth into the world for the benefit of those who can discern its meaning.[48]

For the reader who wants a shorter and simpler, but accurate, version of the *I Ching* that has inherent value, because it has been translated only once (Chinese to English), rather than twice, as was the case with the Wilhelm/Baynes *I Ching* (Chinese to German and then to English), I recommend John Blofeld's *I Ching*.[49] One of the first innovations Blofeld makes is to call his *I Ching* the *Book of Change*. He focuses on "the process of change" rather than individual changes. Blofeld lauds Jung because he "courageously dared the scorn of his fellow scientists by publicly asserting his belief in the *I Ching*'s predictions."[50] Blofeld adds, "His scientist's integrity was revealed by his willingness to jeopardize his reputation among his fellow scientists rather then suppress what seemed to him to be the [truth]."[51]

Blofeld writes about the Tao (which has its source in the *I Ching* or, more accurately, the over three-thousand-year-old *Book of Change* has its origin in the Tao):

Tao is very often the Way that each individual has to follow if [one person] wishes to accord with the great cosmic principles that govern life instead of putting up a futile resistance to them at the cost of needless stress and frustration.[52]

Blofeld continues:

Closely associated with the loftiest connotation of Tao is the concept of Te which, in its primary sense, is the functioning or power of the Tao within the mind of an individual. If I empty my mind of its likes and dislikes together with all the other rubbish accumulated during a lifetime of folly, I may expect to be guided by the universal Tao in me, that is to say by my personal Te. From this concept is derived another of Te's meaning—virtue, both in its moral sense and in the sense of a specific power as when we speak of a [person] . . . as possessing the virtue of healing.[53]

In contrast to Blofeld's choice of "virtue"[54] for translation of "Te," I favor Victor Mair's rendering of "Te" as "integrity."[55] The reason I like Mair's translation of "Te" as "integrity" is that it fits so well with the Tao of Jung and his psychology, which are inseparable. Already Blofeld has spoken of Jung's "scientist's integrity," which I would shorten—in the spirit of change—to simply "integrity." "Integrity" means "spiritual wholeness," and it is my view that Jung embodied integrity during the final phase of his life.

As Lao Tzu says:

The Way alone is good at beginning
and good at completing.[56]

One of the most awe-inspiring aspects of the Chinese way of life is the manner in which they honor family—particularly children, the elderly, and their ancestors. Jung also developed this Chinese or Taoist view toward his family, as well as his known and unknown ancestral heritage.

Honoring the Dead

Like a Chinese Taoist, Jung venerated his ancestors. The place where he did this was at Bollingen. As Jung said, "The Tower, . . . is connected with the dead.[57] He started to build the first tower shortly after his mother died in 1923, and the last part of Bollingen was added soon after his wife died in 1955 (see plate 19). Jung carved his ancestors' names on stone tablets, and during the process said:

PLATES 18 AND 19.
The first and final Towers
The first Tower, built in 1923

The Towers in 1956

I became aware of the fateful links between me and my ancestors. I feel very strongly that I am under the influence of things or questions which were left incomplete and unanswered by my parents and grandparents and more distant ancestors. It often seems as if there were an impersonal karma within a family, which is passed on from parents to children. It has always seemed to me that I had to answer questions which fate had posed to my forefathers, and which had not yet been answered, or as if I had to complete, or perhaps continue, things which previous ages had left unfinished.[58]

He continued:

Our souls as well as our bodies are composed of individual elements which were all already present in the ranks of our ancestors. The "newness" in the individual psyche is an endlessly varied recombination of age-old components. Body and soul therefore have an intensely historical character and find no proper place in what is new, in things that have just come into being. That is to say, our ancestral components are only partly at home in such things.[59]

Furthermore, Jung stated:

Thus we remain ignorant of whether our ancestral components find an elementary gratification in our lives, or whether they are repelled. Inner peace and contentment depend in large measure upon whether or not the historical family which is inherent in the individual can be harmonized with the ephemeral condition of the present.[60]

Jung concluded:

In the Tower at Bollingen it is as if one lived in many centuries simultaneously. The place will outlive me, and in its location and style it points backward to things of long ago. There is very little about it to suggest the present. If a man of the sixteenth century were to move into the house, only the kerosene lamp and the matches would be new to him; otherwise, he would know his way about without difficulty. There is nothing to disturb the dead, neither electric light nor telephone. More over, my ancestors' souls are sustained by the atmosphere of the house, since I answer for them the questions that their lives once left behind. I carve out rough answers as best I can. I have even drawn them on the walls. It is as if a silent, greater family, stretching down the centuries, were peopling the house. There I live in my second personality and see life in the round, as something forever coming into being and passing on.[61]

Clearly, Jung adhered to this maxim of Lao Tzu's:

Just realize where you come from:
This is the essence of wisdom.[62]

Jung's honoring of the dead at Bollingen, which he considered a maternal yin place—by the lakeside, in a valley—was intricately connected to creativity. In fact, his first heart attack proved to be a transformation in Jung's creative work. As he said:

After the illness a fruitful period of work began for me. A good many of my principal works were written only then. The insight I had had, or the vision of the end of all things, gave me the courage to undertake new formulations. I no longer attempted to put across my own opinion, but surrendered myself to the current of my thoughts. Thus one problem after the other revealed itself to me and took shape.[63]

Jung had experienced and then embodied Lao Tzu's wise words:

The spirit of the valley never dies.
It is called "the [mysterious] female."
The gateway of the dark female
is called "the root of Heaven and Earth,"
Uninterrupted as though persistent
it is effective without effort.[64]

Chu Hsi said:

The female is one who receives something and, with it, creates. This creative principle is the most marvelous thing in the universe.[65]

The Stone

Remember: Jung's boyhood experience of sitting on the stone and the question that arose very much like a Zen koan: "Am I the one who is sitting on the stone, or am I the stone on which *he* is sitting?"[66]

Recall: The teenage Jung "brooding on the secret" of God's defecation on, and the shattering of, the Basel Cathedral. Again, Jung sat on the stone and "Whenever [he] thought that [he] was the stone, the conflict eased."[67] Jung thought, "The stone has no uncertainties, no urge to communicate, and is eternally the same for thousands of years."[68] Jung intuitively knew, "the Other [No. 2 personality] in [him] was the timeless, imperishable stone."[69]

Recollect: When at the gymnasium, Jung felt a "kinship with stone" that "*was* the bottomless mystery of being, the embodiment of spirit."[70]

At the age of seventy-five, Jung carved the famous Bollingen Stone (see plate 20). Here he gives the account:

In 1950 I made a kind of monument out of stone to express what the Tower means to me. The story of how this stone came to me is a curious one. I needed stones for building the enclosing wall for the so-called garden, and ordered them from the quarry near Bollingen. I was standing by when the mason gave all the measurements to the owner of the quarry, who wrote them down in his notebook. When the stones arrived by ship and were unloaded, it turned out that the cornerstone had altogether the wrong measure-

PLATE 20.
View of the Tower and the Stone

ments; instead of a triangular stone, a square block had been sent: a perfect cube of much larger dimensions than had been ordered, about twenty inches thick. The mason was furious and told the barge men to take it right back with them.

But when I saw the stone, I said, "No, that is my stone. I must have it!" For I had seen at once that it suited me perfectly and that I wanted to do something with it. Only I did not yet know what.

The first thing that occurred to me was a Latin verse by the alchemist Arnaldus de Villanova (died 1313). I chiseled this into the stone; in translation it goes:

> Here stands the mean, uncomely stone,
> 'Tis very cheap in price!
> The more it is despised by fools,
> The more loved by the wise.

This verse refers to the alchemist's stone, the *lapis,* which is despised and rejected.

Soon something else emerged. I began to see on the front face [see plate 21], in the natural structure of the stone, a small circle, a sort of eye, which looked at me. I chiseled it into the stone, and in the center made a tiny homunculus. This corresponds to the "little doll" (*pupilla*)—yourself— which you see in the pupil of another's eye; a kind of Kabir, or the Telesphoros of Asklepios. Ancient statues show him wearing a hooded cloak and carrying a lantern. At the same time he is a pointer of the way. I dedicated a few words to him which came into my mind while I was working. The inscription is in Greek; the translation goes:

"Time is a child—playing like a child—playing a board game—the kingdom of the child. This is Telesphoros, who roams through the dark regions of this cosmos and glows like a star out of the depths. He points the way to the gates of the sun and to the land of dreams."[71]

These words came to me—one after the other—while I worked on the stone.

On the third face [see plate 22], the one facing the lake, I let the stone itself speak, as it were, in a Latin inscription. These sayings are more or less quotations from alchemy. This is the translation:

"I am an orphan, alone; nevertheless I am found every-

PLATE 21.
The Bollingen Stone (Front face)

where. I am one, but opposed to myself. I am youth and old man at one and the same time. I have known neither father nor mother, because I have had to be fetched out of the deep like a fish, or fell like a white stone from heaven. In woods and mountains I roam, but I am hidden in the innermost soul of man. I am mortal for everyone, yet I am not touched by the cycle of eons."

PLATE 22.
The Bollingen Stone (Lakeside face)

In conclusion, under the saying of Arnaldus de Villanova, I set down in Latin the words, "In remembrance of his seventy-fifth birthday C. G. Jung made and placed this here as a thanks offering, in the year 1950."

When the stone was finished, I looked at it again and again, wondering about it and asking myself what lay behind my impulse to carve it.

The stone stands outside the Tower, and is like an explanation of it. It is a manifestation of the occupant, but one which remains incomprehensible to others. Do you know what I wanted to chisel into the back face of the stone: *"Le cri de Merlin!"* For what the stone expressed reminded me of Merlin's life in the forest, after he had vanished from the world. Men still hear his cries, so the legend runs, but they cannot understand or interpret them.[72]

Lao Tzu is able to illuminate the darkness surrounding the stone and Jung's stone-carving craft:

He is ready to use all situations
and doesn't waste anything.
This is called embodying the light.

A good artist lets his intuition
lead him wherever it wants.[73]

Answer to Job and Synchronicity

The year 1952 proved to be a halcyon one for Jung with the publication of two works, *Answer to Job*[74] and "Synchronicity,"[75] that shattered conventional religious and scientific thought respectively. Because of the controversy surrounding *Answer to Job,* Jung was viewed as a heretic and Gnostic by traditional Christian groups. Jung followed up on the insight he had as a prepubescent lad in Basel by asserting that God was both good and bad. Of course, Taoists had viewed things similarly for over two thousand years. As you may recall, here is what Lao Tzu has to say:

> The Tao doesn't take sides;
> it gives birth to both good and evil.[76]

Another of Jung's equally disputed suppositions is that God wanted to become human (first through Job and then through Jesus Christ) in order to become conscious!

Similarly provocative in the scientific world was Jung's theory of synchronicity. However, when Wolfgang Pauli, the Nobel laureate in physics, co-authored a book with Jung on the subject, *The Interpretation of Nature and the Psyche,*[77] Jung's supposition received more serious attention.

Jung's associations with esteemed physicists and the etiology of synchronicity goes back to the first decade of this century. Jung's theory of synchronicity owes its origin in part to Albert Einstein, who, like Jung, was a professor in Zürich at the time. Recorded in a letter,[78] it was a dinner party at Jung's home in Küsnacht that brought them together. Jung used to host such events composed of Zürich scholars of varying disciplines on a regular basis. At one of these dinners, Jung asked Einstein if his innovative theories in modern physics, which concerned relativity and outer space, could equally apply to the realm of the psyche, that is, inner space. Einstein thought it was feasible. In his affirmation, Einstein was an unknowing midwife to one of the most intriguing concepts in modern psychology.

In formulating the theory of synchronicity, Jung embodied one of Lao Tzu's precepts:

> A good scientist has freed himself of concepts
> and keeps his mind open to what is.[79]

Jung expanded his initial view of synchronicity (meaningful coincidences) to a much broader natural principle, which he called "acausal orderedness,"[80] which sounds a lot like chaos theory.[81] Acausal orderedness occurs in an ongoing way in nature, but synchronistic events are acts of creation at specific moments in time. It is significant that James Gleick notes, "Those studying chaotic dynamics discovered that the disorderly behavior of simple systems acts as a creative process."[82]

Regarding synchronicity, Hannah notes that:

While Jung was writing [about] synchronicity, he also carved the face of the laughing trickster in the west wall of the original Tower [see plate 23]. It was almost as if the images lay dormant in the stones themselves, asking to be brought into existence.[83]

Loss of Outer Feminine and Deepening Inner Feminine

The shock of Toni Wolff's death in March 1953 caused a relapse in Jung's own health, uncontrolled tachycardia (which kept him away from the funeral). Jung was helped in his mourning process by seeing Toni in a dream on the subsequent Easter Eve. As recorded by Hannah, "He saw just her image, there was no action in the dream."[84] Hannah also says:

Although it took Jung a long time to overcome the shock physically, he was able much sooner to find a psychological attitude to Toni's death and to accept the pain it gave him.[85]

Nevertheless, it is my contention that Toni Wolff's death somehow freed Jung to deepen his own inner well of creative feminine. It was as if the loss of one of his two main outer anima

PLATE 23.
The laughing trickster

figures (Emma being the other) actually allowed Jung's creative muse to become more animated! He was able to make great progress on *Mysterium Coniunctionis,* which he completed in 1954, the year before Emma died.

Although Jung wrote in the first sentence of his foreword to *Mysterium Coniunctionis* that this would be his "last book," it wasn't. Most significant is the fact that it was completed in 1954, the year sandwiched between the deaths of the two most important women in his life. (The subtitle for *Mysterium Coniunctionis* is noteworthy: *An Inquiry into the Separation and Synthesis of Psychic Opposites in Alchemy.*) Jung worked on this magnificent work from 1941 to 1954, but he was only able to finish it after Toni Wolff's death. By completing this work, Jung also came much closer to being Taoist. Jung stated the *Mysterium Coniunctionis* "is nothing less than a restoration of the original state of the cosmos and the divine unconsciousness of the world. . . . It is the western equivalent of the fundamental principle of classical Chinese philosophy, namely the union of yang and yin in *Tao.*"[86]

In the interim between Toni's death and Emma's, Jung was able to enjoy a renewed union with his wife, one that mirrored what he had just written about, that is, the *coniunctio* or alchemical marriage that is the final step leading to the transformative gold or philosopher's stone.

Though it is difficult to summarize Jung's alchemical opus in a short space, I will attempt to here. The first stage (of three) is to save the dark opposite from oblivion by uniting it with the light opposite, which is called *unio mentalis*. This coincides with becoming conscious of one's shadow. As Chuang Tzu put it: "In the deep dark the person alone sees light."[87] Jung characterized it in this way (when commenting on the ancient Chinese Taoist alchemical work *The Secret of the Golden Flower*): "darkness gives birth to light."[88] The second stage of *Mysterium Coniunctionis* is a "chemical marriage" uniting the highest heaven (male) with the lowest earth (female). The third and final stage is the union with the *Unus Mundus* (ego-Self and self-Self or Tao axis/connection.) It is actualized in the individual as Te or integrity, which is the same as spiritual wholeness.

In this great work (*Mysterium Coniunctionis*), Jung equates the "alchemical operation"—the symbolic rite performed in the laboratory (which parallels the analytic process or individuation)—with "active imagination." The critical task is to create an image or creative product that unifies the opposites, which is the catalyst or the transcendent function leading to harmony, spiritual wholeness, or integrity.

After Emma died, in November 1955, Jung was profoundly depressed. However, he managed to lead his large extended family into the local church for the funeral service in Küsnacht. Regarding Emma's death, Jung wrote:

I felt an inner obligation to become what I myself am. To put it in the language of the Bollingen house, I suddenly realized that the small central section which crouched so low, so hidden, was myself! I could no longer hide myself behind the "maternal" and the "spiritual" towers. So, in that same year, I added an upper story to this section, which represents myself, or my ego-personality (see plate 19). Earlier, I would not have been able to do this; I would have regarded it as presumptuous self-emphasis. Now it signified an extension of consciousness achieved in old age. With that the building was complete. . . . It gave me a feeling as if I were being reborn in stone. It is thus a concretization of the individuation process, a memorial *aera perennius*. . . . I built the house in sections, always following the concrete needs of the moment. It might also be said that I built it in a kind of dream. Only afterward did I see how all the parts fitted together and that a meaningful form had resulted: a symbol of psychic wholeness.[89]

Lao Tzu's perspective is similar:

The master views the parts with compassion,
because he understands the whole.
His constant practice is humility.
He doesn't glitter like a jewel
but lets himself be shaped by the Tao,
as rugged and common as a stone.[90]

Franz Jung (Jung's only son) told me that his father was extremely depressed for over five months after his mother's death. He and his sisters suggested that their father draw again (as he had done in the *Red Book*). He attempted this in pencil, but was unable to pursue it. Franz found out that, as with Bollingen, his father had to work in stone. So Franz got him a stone tablet about eighteen by thirty inches, and Jung carved both sides. On the outer face, he carved a graceful branch of a ginkgo tree coming out of the lower-left quadrant and going into the upper-right—it had five leaves and one was falling. Franz showed this stonework to me; there is a little old Chinese man in the bottom lower-right quadrant. There are also five Chinese characters on the left panel, which translate as "Man in modest harmony with nature." In addition, on the reverse side, he carved Latin letters that read in English as: "Offered to the Gods with my hands, made and placed here by C. G. Jung, 1956." This tablet was put under a ginkgo tree at Küsnacht, which was given to Jung in 1956 by the American students at the Jung Institute in memory of his wife. It stayed there for thirty-seven years, but in 1993, it was brought inside, chipped and weather-worn.

Since this is not the first time that Jung identified with being a moderate man, let's see what Lao Tzu has to say:

> there is nothing better than moderation.

> The mark of a moderate man
> is freedom from his own ideas.
> Tolerant like the sky,
> all-pervading like sunlight,
> firm like a mountain,
> supple like a tree in the wind,
> he has no distraction in view
> and makes use of anything
> life happens to bring his way.

> Nothing is impossible for him.
> Because he has let go.[91]

The Final Years: Finding Purpose and Meaning

After his wife's death, Jung wrote in a letter that it helped him most *not* to dwell on the past, but to concentrate on *why* he had to be the survivor and to give his whole energy to finding the purpose he still had to fulfill.[92]

He was quite willing to face the fact that it was in a way a merciful fate that had forced him to survive both Toni and Emma, because, as he proved in the five and a half years that elapsed before his own death, he was able to go on *creatively* with his life and his individuation process after losing them.[93]

Jung relied on his own creative anima more and more, but he attributed much to Emma's death:

> Everything that I have written in 1957 and in 1956 ["Why and How I wrote my Answer to Job," "The Undiscovered Self," "Flying Saucers: A Modern Myth," "A Psychological View of Conscience," and work on *Memories, Dreams, Reflections*] has grown out of the stone sculptures I did after my wife's death [see plate 24]. The close of her life, the end, and what it made me realize, wrenched me violently out of myself. It cost me a great deal to regain my footing, and contact with stone helped me.[94]

Also, a dream Jung had of his wife "looking more beautiful than ever," which is recorded in a letter to Laurens van der Post, helped to transform Jung's depression following his wife's death.[95]

The Supreme Being: A Gnostic Experience

In 1959, John Freeman, in the famous *Face to Face* BBC interview of Jung, asked him if he believed in God. Jung paused, and then said, "I don't believe, I know." Jung knew the Supreme Being just as he knew that "only the wounded physician heals,"[96] by experience. Jung also realized that he was a part of an ongoing mystery of meaning, which we could call the Tao.

> Human consciousness created objective existence and meaning, and man found his indispensable place in the great process of being.[97]

PLATE 24.
Stone carving in memory of Emma Jung (Next to the Loggia)

In fact, Jung concurred with Wilhelm's translation of the *Tao* as "meaning." Jung amplified this as follows:

Just as Wilhelm gave the spiritual treasure of the East a . . . meaning, so we should translate this meaning into life. To do this—that is, to realize *Tao*—would be the true task. . . .

I know our unconscious is full of Eastern symbolism. The spirit of the East is really at our gates. Therefore it seems to me that the search for *Tao*, for a meaning in life, has already become a collective phenomenon among us, and to a far greater extent than is generally realized.[98]

Jung knew that "the decisive question for man is: Is he related to something infinite or not?"99 Additionally, Jung discerned that "the sole purpose of human existence is to kindle a light in the darkness of mere being."100

In 1960, after his eighty-fifth birthday, Jung became seriously ill. He told Barbara Hannah and Marie-Louise von Franz the following dream, which signaled his coming death. He dreamed of

the "other Bollingen" bathed in a glow of light, and a voice told him that it was now completed and ready for habitation. Then far below he saw a mother wolverine teaching her child to dive and swim in a stretch of water.101

As had happened before, Jung recovered from this bout of illness (see plate 25). He then wrote "Approaching the Unconscious" for the planned book *Man and His Symbols*,102 which has done so much to popularize Jung's work.

Once Jung was speaking with Barbara Hannah regarding reincarnation and she said that she hoped this would be the last time she had to reincarnate. Hannah subsequently said:

Jung began to agree with me warmly . . . but then he suddenly stopped and looked around in silence. Then he said: "No, I am wrong. If I might have Bollingen I would be willing to come back again."103

By design, Jung's spirit lives on at Bollingen in stone!

Looking Back and Looking Ahead

In the last two pages of *Memories, Dreams, Reflections,* Jung states:

I am satisfied with the course my life has taken. . . . Much might have been different if I myself had been different. But

PLATE 25.
Jung at Küsnacht, 1960

it was as it had to be; for all came about because I am as I
am . . . I regret many follies which sprang from my obsti-
nacy; but without that trait, I would not have reached my
goal. And so I am disappointed and not disappointed. . . . I
am astonished [and] . . . pleased with myself. I am distressed,
depressed, rapturous. I am all these things at once, and cannot add up the sum. . . . Life is—or has—meaning and
meaninglessness. I cherish the anxious hope that meaning
will preponderate and win the battle.[104]

Marie-Louise von Franz[105] maintained that in his last decade,
Jung vowed not to identify with any archetype, especially that of
the wise old man, which he had defined as the *"archetype of meaning."*[106] The above statement "Life is—or has—meaning and
meaninglessness" suggests that Marie-Louise von Franz was correct: Jung did not identify with either pole of the archetype, neither positive (meaning) nor negative (meaninglessness), but rather

conceived of both possibilities. Therefore, Jung was consciously holding the tension of the opposites for the wise old man archetype (which I also see as the Taoist master archetype), and here it was clearly in the service of the Tao and his individuation process.

It is significant that Jung closes his autobiography with a quote by Lao Tzu: "All are clear, I alone am clouded." Here he comes very close to using that ancient Taoist sage as his personal Master. Jung explains:

> He is expressing what I now feel in advanced old age. [Lao Tzu] is the example of a man with superior insight who has seen and experienced worth and worthlessness, and who at the end of his life desires to return into his own being, into the eternal unknowable meaning. The archetype of the old man who has seen enough is eternally true. . . . The more uncertain I have felt about myself, the more there has grown up in me a feeling of kinship with all things. In fact it seems to me as if that alienation which so long separated me from the world has become transferred into my own inner world, and has revealed to me an unexpected unfamiliarity with myself.[107]

Related to Jung's closing reflection, I am reminded of another Taoist master's, Chuang Tzu's, wise statement:

> When there is separation, there is coming together. When there is coming together, there is dissolution. All things may become one, whatever their state of being. Only he who has transcended sees this oneness. He has no use for differences and dwells in the constant. To be constant is to be useful . . . To be useful is to realize one's true nature. Realization of one's true nature is happiness. When one reaches happiness, one is close to perfection. So one stops, yet does not know that one stops. This is Tao.[108]

Jung puts it all together in another piece written just three years before he died. He links Judeo-Christian symbolism with Taoism. Jung said:

> The Chinese symbol of the *one* [Being], Tao, consists of *yang* (fire, hot, dry, south side of the mountain, masculine, etc.) and *yin* (dark, moist, cool, north side of the mountain, feminine, etc.). It fully corresponds, therefore, to the Jewish symbol [the "star of David," ✡, which consists of △ =fire and ▽ =water. The hexad is a totality symbol: 4 as the natural division of the circle, 2 as the vertical axis (zenith and nadir)—a spatial conception of totality]. . . . The Christian equivalent can be found in the Church's doctrine of one unity of mother and son and in the androgyny of Christ.[109]

Furthermore, Jung realized, in one of the last things he wrote, that "the Self is . . . like Tao, [that] is, 'psychic totality.' "[119]

As the sun was setting on Jung's human life, he adhered to Lao Tzu's wisdom:

> If you stay in the center
> and embrace death with your whole heart,
> you will endure forever.[111]

> He holds nothing back from life;
> therefore he is ready for death,
> as a man is ready for sleep
> after a good day's work.[112]

> Seeing into darkness is clarity.
> Knowing how to yield is strength.
> Use your own light
> and return to the source of light.
> This is called practicing eternity.[113]

Jung's last dream, a few nights before his death, is a clear indication that he had actualized his potential and was about to reunite with the Tao and Self. The dream has three parts, in which Jung saw:

1) A big, round block of stone in a high bare place and on it was inscribed: "This shall be a sign unto you of wholeness and oneness."

2) [Many] vessels—pottery vases—on the right side of a square place.

3) [This place,] a square of trees, contained fibrous roots coming up from the ground and surrounding him. There were gold threads . . . gleaming among the roots.[114]

It was fitting that a stone carried the message; You are one with all, feminine containers were available to Jung, indicating he was ready to receive the spirit, and he was within the four sides of a square of trees (a *Temenos*), surrounded by roots and golden threads. Jung had become part of the Secret of the Golden Trees and firmly rooted in Mother Earth.

During his final years, Jung embodied "the actionless action, called by the Chinese *Wu Wei*";[115] this is the same thing as being spontaneously reborn in spirit. As Thomas Merton characterized it: "One breaks through the limits of cultural structural religion . . . [where one experiences] a kind of limitlessness. . . . lack of inhibition, . . . psychic fullness of creativity, which mark the fully integrated maturity of the 'enlightened self.' "[116]

Martin Buber (who also lived in the spirit of the Tao) says, "The decisive heart searching is the beginning of the way in man's life."[117] He adds, "Every man's foremost task is the actualization of his unique, unprecedented and never-recurring potentialities."[118] Buber then advocates union of body and spirit through nature[119] (something that Jung spent a lifetime realizing). In the same vein as Jung's thesis in *Answer to Job*, Buber says, "God wishes to come to his world, but he wants to come to it through man."[120] Therefore, as Buber declares, "This is the ultimate purpose: to [provide] . . . a dwelling for the Divine Presence."[121] Both Buber and Jung serve as examples for us. Lao Tzu, likewise a model, gives us the basic truth:

Let the Tao be present in your life
and you will become genuine.
Whoever is planted in the Tao
will not be rooted up.[122]

These three [things] are your greatest treasures:
simplicity, patience, [and] compassion.[123]

Cultivated in the person, integrity is true.[124]

Epilogue

To see things in the seed, that is genius.

LAO TZU

Now we've come full circle—the end is the beginning. Ending this book represents an opening and a new beginning. Jung's spirit lives on, as his psychology grows golden blossoms and bears fruit. He planted seeds far and wide around the world, which will mature and develop over the years. The following quote, with which Jung opens "A Study in the Process of Individuation,"[1] is a fitting testimonial to the Tao and "the Tao of Jung":

Tao's working of things is vague and obscure.
Obscure! Oh vague!
In it are images.
Vague! Oh obscure!

In it are things.
Profound! Oh dark indeed!
In it a seed.
Its seed is [the] very truth.
In it is trustworthiness.
From the earliest Beginning until today
Its name is not lacking
By which to fathom the Beginning of all things.
How do I know it is the Beginning of all things?
Through *it!*

—Lao Tzu[2]

A Closing Reflection

In the Preface, I said that writing this book represented a turning point in my life. I was naïve[3] when I went to Switzerland, but it was not the first time and probably it won't be the last. I truly thought the heart would grow fonder. However, it takes two hearts growing fonder to make a marriage work. I thought the crisis would be resolved: the danger dealt with and the opportunity realized. I thought my marriage would not only survive but that it would individuate. I concur with Adolph Guggenbühl-Craig's thesis in *Marriage: Dead or Alive*[4] that a marriage, like a person, individuates (grows and develops) and actualizes itself. In other words, a marriage is not to be terminated prematurely (of course, over half of them are!). To do so would be like the ultimate trickster act of the ego in ending one's own life. Divorce, also an act of the ego, can be seen in the same light. To make a long story short, my wife (without reading the copy of *Marriage: Dead or Alive* that I'd sent her) pronounced our marriage dead. Shortly after I returned to Texas, she filed for divorce.[5] Ironically, but meaningfully, the divorce (the parting or, more accurately, the loss and death) occurred on Halloween. Therefore, in an archetypal sense, I became involved in a massive trick or treat. Despite the pain and hardship, I'm determined to focus on the treat and retreat. I'm no longer bound to a specific person or way of life. Increasingly, my ex-wife had viewed my writing as a mistress. As my prophetic dream on the eve of my departure to Switzerland indicated, I was with my muse, but in reality she posed no threat to my ex-wife. Nevertheless, while my outer marriage dissolved, an inner union with my anima was consummated.

As Toni Morrison has said, "The function of freedom is to free someone else." My freedom allowed me to free my muse to write this book, but it cost me my marriage. However, in my opinion, it also freed my ex-wife from what she must have considered an unacceptable situation. I lived through the crisis and unlike my inclination to suicide when my first marriage collapsed,[6] this time I ended up experiencing egocide and transformation or practicing what I've been preaching.

The end result of it all is to forgive. I've freed up my anima—my soul—in order to write a book about Jung and ultimately about forgiving him. This book is also about forgiving myself and my ex-wife. In addition, I realize that what I've done is a model for my three daughters—it's a model of freedom, forgiveness, and individuation. It is meaningful that this book closes with a breath of fresh air. *The Tao of Jung* is dedicated to my oldest daughter, Sarah, who is now an art major at the University of Texas in Austin. During the fall of 1994, she took a risk and applied to work at the Fresh Air Fund camp outside of New York City, where inner-city kids spend a summer in the country with plenty of fresh air to breathe, a lake to swim in, gardens to tend, farm animals to care for, art to make, and wilderness walks to be taken. In the spring of 1995, when this book was going into production, she found out that she was accepted, and during the summer of 1995 she was a counselor and a teacher of pottery for girls seven to twelve years of age. I'm certain that this experience will have an impact on her future: her relationships and vocational options. At the tender age of nineteen, she has taken a Confucian step leading to a thousand new pathways. The function of her freedom, like Lao Tzu's, Jung's, mine, and yours, is to free someone else.

Chronology
of Jung's Life

℞ *1. Sunrise to the Eve of Pubescence*

1875   Born July 26 in Kesswil, Switzerland. Six months later moves to Laufen, near the Rhine Falls and across from Schaffhausen.

1879   Moves to Klein-Hüningen, near Basel.

1884   Birth of sister.

1886   Starts schooling at the Basel Gymnasium.

⌈ *2. Puberty to Psychiatry*

1895–1900   Attends the University of Basel and studies the natural sciences and medicine.

1896   Death of father.

1900   Chooses psychiatry and moves to Zürich to study and work at the Burghölzli Mental Hospital under Eugen Bleuler.

1902   Dissertation (University of Zürich): *On the Psychology and Pathology of So-called Occult Phenomena.*

1903   Marries Emma Rauschenbach.

1905   Appointed Lecturer in Medicine (Psychiatry) at the University of Zürich.

₹ 3. The Freud Years

1906   Supports Freud's psychoanalysis and begins correspondence with Freud.

1907   First meeting with Freud in Vienna.

1908   Attends first International Congress of Psycho-Analysis in Vienna.

1909   Journey to America with Freud to give Clark University lectures.

1910   Attends Second International Congress of Psycho-Analysis in Nuremberg and appointed permanent president.

1912   Publishes *The Psychology of the Unconscious (Symbols of Transformation).*

1913   Break with Freud.

   Resigns academic position, University of Zürich.

1914   Resigns presidency of International Congress of Psycho-Analysis.

✗ 4. Creative Illness

1914–16   Inward awakening.

1916   Paints first mandala.

   Writes *Seven Sermons to the Dead.*

   Publishes *Collected Papers on Analytical Psychology.*

1918   Recognition of the Self as goal of psychic development.

1921   Publishes *Psychological Types.*

1922   Purchases Bollingen property.

1923   Death of mother. Work starts on Bollingen Tower.

1924 Visit to Taos pueblo, New Mexico.

1925 Trip to Africa (Mount Elgon).

1926 Returns from Africa via Egypt.

❀ 5. *Union of East and West*

1928 Collaborates with Richard Wilhelm on a Taoist alchemical text: *The Secret of the Golden Flower.*

Publishes *The Spiritual Problem of Modern Man.*

1930 Becomes vice-president of the General Medical Society for Psychotherapy.

1933 Hitler becomes German chancellor.

Kretschmer resigns as president of the General Medical Society for Psychotherapy and Jung takes over.

Appointed Lecturer at Eidgenössische Technische Hochschule, Zürich.

1935 Gives Tavistock lectures: "Analytical Psychology: Its Theory and Practice."

Writes psychological commentary to *The Tibetan Book of the Dead.*

1936 Receives honorary doctorate from Harvard.

1937 Gives Terry lectures at Yale University: "Psychology and Religion."

1938 Receives honorary doctorate from Oxford.

Journey to India.

1939 Writes psychological commentary to *The Tibetan Book of the Great Liberation* and a foreword to Suzuki's *Introduction to Zen Buddhism.*

1942 Resigns post at Eidgenössische Technische Hochschule.

1943 Accepts Chair (professorship) in Medical Psychology at the University of Basel.

1944 Suffers a serious heart attack and illness forces resignation from Basel professorship.

1945 Receives honorary doctorate from University of Geneva on his seventieth birthday.

Writes "After the Catastrophe."

1946 Suffers second heart attack—this not as serious as first.

Writes "The Fight with the Shadow."

❧6. Sunset and Return to the Self

1947 Retires to Bollingen Tower.

1948 Approves the establishment of the C. G. Jung Institute in Zürich.

1950 Writes a foreword to the *I Ching*.

1952 Publishes work on synchronicity and *Answer to Job*.

1953 Jung's *Collected Works* are published in the United States.

Toni Wolff dies.

1955 Receives honorary degree from the Eidgenössische Technische Hochschule on his eightieth birthday.

Death of Emma Jung.

Publishes *Mysterium Coniunctionis*.

1957 Begins work with Aniela Jaffé on his autobiography, *Memories, Dreams, Reflections*.

Writes *The Undiscovered Self (Present and Future)*.

1958 Writes "Flying Saucers: A Modern Myth."

1959 Writes "Good and Evil in Analytical Psychology."

1960 Begins work on *Man and His Symbols*.

1961 Jung dies after a brief illness, June 6, at his home in Küsnacht.

Notes

Preface

1. Jung, C. G. (1973) *C. G. Jung Letters*, vol.1: 1906–1950. Selected and edited by Gerhard Adler, in collaboration with Aniela Jaffé. Trans. R. F. C. Hull. Princeton: Princeton University Press, p. 559.
2. Jaffé, A. (1972) *From the Life and Work of C. G. Jung*. Trans. R. F. C. Hull. London: Hodder & Stoughton, pp. 132–33

Introduction

1. *The I Ching*. (1967) 3d ed. Trans. R. Wilhelm (German) and C. F. Baynes (English). Bollingen Series XIX. Princeton: Princeton University Press, p. 98.
2. Jung, C. G. (1968) *The Collected Works of C. G. Jung (CW)*, vol. 13, *Alchemical Studies*. Trans. R. F. C. Hull, eds. Sir Herbert Read, Michael Fordham, Gerhard Adler, and William McGuire, executive editor. Bollingen Series XX. Princeton: Princeton University Press, p. 83.
3. Jean Shinoda Bolen has described the Tao as both synchronicity and the Self (see *The Tao of Psychology*, 1979 San Francisco: Harper & Row). However, in my view, the Tao is simply the Self, the center and the totality.
4. Jung, C. G. (1973) *C. G. Jung Letters*, vol. 1, p. 560.

Chapter 1

1. Jung, C. G. (1942/1954) "Transformation Symbolism in the Mass," in *CW*, vol. 11, *Psychology and Religion: West and East*, p. 259.

2. Jung, C. G. (1963) *Memories, Dreams, Reflections (MDR)*. New York: Pantheon, p. 326.

3. Jung, C. G. *MDR*, p. 4.

4. Jung, C. G. *MDR*, p. 6.

5. Lao Tzu. (1972) *Tao Te Ching (TTC)*. Trans. G-F. Feng and J. English. New York: Vintage Books, no. 28.

6. Chuang Tzu. (1974) *Inner Chapters (IC)*. Trans. G-F. Feng and J. English. New York: Vintage Books, p. 68.

7. Jung, C. G. *MDR*, p. 7.

8. Lao Tzu. (1988) *TTC*. Trans. S. Mitchell. New York: Harper-Collins, no. 8.

9. Jung, C. G. *MDR*, pp. 19–20. The stone became a lifelong preoccupation of Jung's. After I had noted this healing quest of Jung's, I came across an excellent article on this subject by Frances Baruch in *Mantis* 4, no. 1 (Winter 1991): 20–33.

10. Jung, C. G. *MDR*, p. 20.

11. Chuang Tzu. *IC*, p. 48.

12. Jung, C. G. *MDR*, p. 20.

13. Lao Tzu. *TTC*, Mitchell, no. 7.

14. Jung, C. G. *MDR*, p. 21.

15. Jung, C. G. *MDR*, p. 23.

16. Jung, C. G. *MDR*, p. 22.

17. Jung, C. G. *MDR*, p. 27.

18. Jung, C. G. *MDR*, p. 30.

19. Jung, C. G. *MDR*, pp. 31–32.

20. Jung, C. G. *MDR*, pp. 32–33.

21. Chuang Tzu. *IC*, p. 74.

22. Chuang Tzu. *IC*, p. 30.

23. All names and descriptions of Tao are cited in Lao Tzu's *TTC*, trans. R. Wilhelm and H. G. Ostwald. (1985) London: Arkana, pp. 5, 12–13, except for the last six, which are from Thomas Cleary's new translation of *The Secret of the Golden Flower*. (SGF-C) (1991) San Francisco: Harper, pp. 9, 14, 81. The term Wilhelm used for the Tao is "meaning."

24. The reference to the descriptions of the Self are from Carl Jung, *CW*, Vol. 7, pp. 175, 238; *CW*, Vol. 12, p. 41; *CW*, Vol. 11, p. 190. The final description (Supreme Being) is my own, see D. Rosen, (1996), *Transforming Depression*. New York: Penguin/Arkana, pp. 67, 68.

25. See *The Secret of the Golden Flower: A Chinese Book of Life*. (*SGF-W*) (1962) Trans. R. Wilhelm and C. F. Barnes. Commentary by C. G. Jung. New York: Harvest/Harcourt Brace Jovanovich, pp. 78, 99–104.

Chapter 2

1. From Shuo Kua's discussion of the trigrams, in this case Kén (Mountain) Keeping Still. *The I Ching*. Trans. Wilhelm and Baynes, p. 271.

2. Chuang Tzu. (1992) "Readings from Chuang Tzu," in T. Merton's *The Way of Chuang Tzu (WCT)*. Boston and London: Shambhala, p. 147.

3. Jung, C. G. *MDR*, p. 36.

4. Jung, C. G. *MDR*, p. 37.

5. Jung, C. G. *MDR*, p. 39.

6. Jung, C. G. *MDR*, pp. 40–42.

7. Jung, C. G. *MDR*, p. 23.

8. Jung, C. G. *MDR*, pp. 11–13. Only much later in his life did Jung realize that the phallus was a common deity figure in the East, and (as noted in *MDR*, p. 13) in Greek "phallus" means "shining, bright."

9. Jung, C. G. *MDR*, p. 41.

10. Jung, C. G. *MDR*, p. 56.

11. Lao Tzu. (1985) *Tao Te Ching (TTC)*, Wilhelm and Ostwald, no. 56, p. 52.
Chuang Tzu also commented on this: "What can be seen by seeing is forms and colors; what can be heard by hearing is names and sounds. How sad! Men of the world think that forms, colors, names, and sounds are adequate means to grasp the full feel of things. But forms, colors, names, and sounds are not adequate to grasp full feel of things. 'He who knows does not speak; he who speaks does not know.' " From *The Complete Works of Chuang Tzu*. (1964) Trans. B. Watson. New York: Columbia University Press, p.489.

12. Jung, C. G. *MDR*, p. 42.

13. Jung, C. G. *MDR*, pp. 44–45.

14. Hall, J. A. (1983) *Jungian Dream Interpretation: A Handbook of Theory and Practice*. Toronto: Inner City Books, p. 28.

15. Lao Tzu. (1988) *TTC*, Mitchell, no. 1.

16. Jung, C. G. (1968) *CW*, vol. 12, *Psychology and Alchemy*, p. 177 in notes.

17. Hall, J. A. (1986) *The Jungian Experience: Analysis and Individuation*. Toronto: Inner City Books, pp. 14–15.

18. Sandner, D., and J. Beebe. (1984) "Psychopathology and Analysis," in M. Stein, ed., *Jungian Analysis*. Boston: Shambhala, pp. 294–334.

19. Neumann, E. (1969) *Depth Psychology and a New Ethic.* Trans. E. Rolfe. New York: G. P. Putnam & Sons, p. 137.

20. Neumann, E. *Depth Psychology and a New Ethic*, p. 138.

21. Lao Tzu. *TTC*, Wilhelm and Ostwald, no. 13, p. 31.

22. Jung, C. G. *MDR*, p. 44.

23. Jung, C. G. *MDR*, p. 8.

24. Anima is the feminine aspect of a man's psyche.

25. Jung, C. G. *MDR*, pp. 8–9.

26. Jung, C. G. *MDR*, p. 9.

27. Jung, C. G. *MDR*, p. 4.

28. Jung, C. G. *MDR*, p. 18.

29. Jung, C. G. *MDR*, pp. 18–19.

30. Lao Tzu. *TTC*, Wilhelm and Ostwald, no. 25, p. 37.

31. From "The Hui Ming Ching" ("The Book of Consciousness and Life"), in *SGF-W*, pp. 77–78.

32. Jung, C. G. *MDR*, pp. 42–43.

33. Jung, C. G. *MDR*, p. 43.

34. Jung, C. G. *MDR*, p. 54.

35. Jung, C. G. *MDR*, p. 55.

36. Jung, C. G. *MDR*, p. 78.

37. Jung, C. G. *MDR*, p. 77.

38. Jung, C. G. *MDR*, pp. 77–78.

39. Chuang Tzu. "Readings from Chuang Tzu," in *WCT*, p. 151.

40. Chuang Tzu. "Readings from Chuang Tzu," in *WCT*, pp. 181, 183.

41. Lao Tzu. (1992) *Wen-tzu: Understanding the Mysteries.* (*Wen-tzu*) Trans. T. Cleary. Boston and London: Shambhala, pp. 173–174.

42. Lao Tzu. *Wen-tzu*, no. 61, p. 55.

43. Lao Tzu. *Wen-tzu*, no. 51, p. 48.

44. Jung, C. G. *MDR*, p. 48.

45. Jung, C. G. *MDR*, p. 57.

46. Jung, C. G. (1952) *Answer to Job,* in *CW* vol. 11, *Psychology and Religion: West and East*, p. 355–470.

47. Jung, C. G. *MDR*, p. 59.

48. Lao Tzu. (1990) *Tao Te Ching: The Classic Book of Integrity and the Way.* (*TTC*) Trans. V. A. Mair. New York: Bantam Books, p. 18.

49. Chuang Tzu. (1992) "Readings from Chuang Tzu," in *WCT*, p. 89.

50. Jung, C. G. *MDR*, p. 59.

51. Lao Tzu. *TTC*, Wilhelm and Ostwald, no. 14, p. 32. S. Mitchell's *TTC* translates it, "Form that included all forms, image without an

image, subtle, beyond all conception," no. 14. And V. Mair's *TTC* version is: "This is called 'the form of the formless, The image of nonentity.' This is called 'the amorphous,' " p. 74.

52. Lao Tzu. *TTC*, Mair, p. 60. Mitchell's *TTC* version is; "When people see some things as good, other things become bad," no. 2. And Wilhelm and Ostwald's *TTC* translation is; "If all on earth acknowledge the good as good, then thereby is the non-good already posited," p. 27.

53. Jung, C. G. *MDR*, p. 68.

54. Jung, C. G. *MDR*, p. 80.

55. Jung, C. G. *MDR*, p. 81.

56. For example, Jung's collaboration with Wilhelm on *The Secret of the Golden Flower* represented an association with Chinese (Taoist) alchemy, whereas Jung's work on European alchemy is well known: *Psychology and Alchemy* (*CW*, vol. 12).

57. Jung, C. G. *MDR*, p. 85.

58. Jung, C. G. *MDR*, p. 72.

59. Jung, C. G. *MDR*, p. 94.

60. Jung, C. G. *MDR*, p. 94.

61. Jung, C. G. *MDR*, p. 96.

62. Jung, C. G. *MDR*, p. 96.

63. Jung, C. G. *MDR*, pp. 87–88.

64. Lao Tzu. *TTC*, Wilhelm and Ostwald, no. 52, p. 50. S. Mitchell's *TTC* (no. 52) is also excellent:

Seeing into darkness is clarity.
Knowing how to yield is strength.
Use your own light
and return to the source of the light.
This is called practicing eternity.

65. Jung, C. G. *MDR*, p. 107.

66. Jung, C. G. *MDR*, pp. 108–9.

67. Lao Tzu. *Wen-tzu*, no. 72, p. 62.

68. Jung, C. G. *MDR*, p. 112.

69. Jung, C. G. *MDR*, p. 113.

70. Chuang Tzu. "The Way of Tao," in "Readings from Chuang Tzu," in *WCT*, p. 137.

71. Chuang Tzu. "Where Is Tao?" in "Readings from Chuang Tzu," in *WCT*, p. 182.

Chapter 3

1. McGuire, W., ed. (1974) *The Freud/Jung Letters (F/J Letters)*. Trans. R. Mannheim and R. F. C. Hull. Bollingen Series XCIV. Princeton: Princeton University Press, p. 28.

2. Jung, C. G. *MDR*, p. 112.

3. Hannah, B. (1976) *Jung, His Life and Work: A Biographical Memoir (J, HL & W)*. New York: G. P. Putnam's Sons, p. 72.

4. Hannah, B. *J, HL & W*, p. 72.

5. "Anima" means "soul" in Latin and in Jung's psychology it is the feminine aspect of a man's psyche. In its development, it is projected onto women. The first to receive the son's anima projection is the mother. Secondly, it goes onto a lover and/or the man's future bride. Thirdly, the anima (and women he is relating to and with) becomes an equal and friend. Fourth and lastly, she becomes man's spiritual companion.

6. Jung, C. G. *MDR*, p. 9.

7. Jung, C. G. (1971) *Erinnerungen, Träume, Gedanken* (German edition of *MDR*). Olten: Walter Verlag, pp. 406–7.

8. Jung, C. G. *Erinnerungen, Träume, Gedanken*, p. 407.

9. From Chang Po-Tuan's classic *Four Hundred Words on the Gold Elixir*, cited by T. Cleary, ed., in *SGF-C*. (1991) San Francisco: Harper, pp. 117–18.

10. Jung, C. G. *MDR*, p. 147.

11. McGuire, W., ed. *F/J Letters*, from the "Introduction," pp. xv, xvi.

12. Jung, C. G. *MDR*, p. 147.

13. McGuire, W., ed. *F/J Letters*, pp. 196–97.

14. McGuire, W., ed. *F/J Letters*, p. 5.

15. McGuire, W., ed. *F/J Letters*, p. xvii.

16. McGuire, W., ed. *F/J Letters*, p. xviii.

17. Recorded as "in February 1907" by Jung in *MDR*, p. 149; however, the correct date is noted by W. McGuire in *The Freud/Jung Letters*, p. 24.

18. Jung, C. G. *MDR*, p. 149.

19. Jung, C. G. *MDR*, p. 149.

20. Jung, C. G. *MDR*, p. 149.

21. McGuire, W., ed. *F/J Letters*, p. 28.

22. McGuire, W., ed. *F/J Letters*, p. 7.

23. Lao Tzu. *Wen-tzu*, no. 39, p. 39.

24. Chuang Tzu. "Readings from Chuang Tzu," in *WCT*, p. 56.

25. Lü, Tung-pin. *SGF-C*, p. 79.

26. McGuire, W., ed. *F/J Letters*, p. 12.

27. Lao Tzu. *Wen-tzu*, no. 122, p. 118.

28. Lao Tzu. *Wen-tzu*, no. 122, p. 118.

29. Lü, Tung-pin. *SGF-C*, no. 14, p. 26.

30. Lü, Tung-pin. *SGF-C*, no. 14, p. 97.

31. Jung, C. G. *MDR*, pp. 150–52.

32. Jung, C. G. *MDR*, pp. 154–55.

33. Lao Tzu. *Wen-tzu*, no. 87, p. 75.

34. Lao Tzu. *Wen-tzu*, no. 46, p. 47.

35. Schur, M. (1972) *Freud: Living and Dying.* New York: International Universities Press, pp. 528–29.

36. Jung, C. G. *MDR*, p. 157.

37. Jung, C. G. *MDR*, p. 361.

38. Jung, C. G. *MDR*, p. 158.

39. Billinsky, J. M. "Jung and Freud: The End of a Romance." *Andover Newton Quarterly,* 10 (1969): 39–43.

40. Jung, C. G. *MDR*, p. 159.

41. Lao Tzu. *Wen-tzu*, no. 53, p. 50.

42. *SGF-W*, p. 60.

43. From Jung's commentary to *SGF-W*, p. 102.

44. Lao Tzu. *Wen-tzu*, no. 41, p. 42.

Chapter 4

1. Jung, C. G. *MDR*, p. 199.

2. Lao Tzu. *TTC*, Mitchell, no. 1. In the same chapter, the Tao is called darkness, the mysterious source.

3. Jung, C. G. *MDR*, p. 179.

4. Jung, C. G. *MDR*, p. 179.

5. Rosen, D. H. (1996) *Transforming Depression: Healing the Soul Through Creativity.* New York: Penguin/Arkana. pp. 61–84.

6. Jung, C. G. *MDR*, p. 180.

7. Jung, C. G. *MDR*, p. 180.

8. Jung, C. G. *MDR*, p. 181.

9. Jung, C. G. *MDR*, p. 181.

10. Jung, C. G. *MDR*, p. 181. The characterization of being on the edge of an abyss is not uncommon. See the cases of Rebecca and Sharon in my book *Transforming Depression*, pp. 108 and 167.

11. Jung, C. G. (1968) *CW*, vol. 9I, *The Archetypes and the Collective Unconscious*, p. 37.

12. Lao Tzu. *TTC*, Mitchell, no. 3.

13. Lao Tzu. *TTC*, Mitchell, no. 4.

14. Lao Tzu. *TTC*, Mitchell, no. 5.

15. Jung, C. G. *MDR*, p. 181.

16. Jung, C. G. *MDR*, p. 182.

17. Jung, C. G. *MDR*, p. 181.

18. Jung, C. G. *MDR*, p. 182.

19. Jung, C. G. *MDR*, p. 182.

20. Jung, C. G. *MDR*, p. 183.

21. Jung, C. G. *MDR*, p. 183.

22. Jung, C. G. *MDR*, p. 183.

23. Jung, C. G. *MDR*, p. 184.

24. Chuang Tzu. "Readings from Chuang Tzu," in *WCT*, pp. 88, 90.

25. Lao Tzu. *TTC*, Mitchell, no. 5.

26. Jung, C. G. *MDR*, pp. 184–85.

27. Jung, C. G. *MDR*, p. 66.

28. Chuang Tzu. "Readings from Chuang Tzu," in *WCT*, p. 102.

29. Lao Tzu. *Wen-tzu*, no. 153, p. 150.

30. Jung, C. G. *MDR*, p. 185.

31. Jung, C. G. *MDR*, p. 185.

32. Carotenuto, A. (1982) *A Secret Symmetry: Sabina Spielrein Between Jung and Freud.* New York: Pantheon Books.

33. Jung, C. G. *MDR*, p. 186.

34. Jung, C. G. *MDR*, p. 186. In the post-Jung era, it is thought that both men and women are androgynous, therefore each person regardless of gender has both anima and animus. See I. C. de Castillejo. (1974) *Knowing Women.* New York: Harper Colophon, pp. 165–82; and V. Kast. (1986) *The Nature of Loving: Patterns of Human Relationship.* Trans. B. Matthews. Wilmette, Il.: Chiron, pp. 87–101.

35. Jung, C. G. *MDR*, appendix V, *Septem Sermones ad Mortuos*, pp. 378–90.

36. Jung, C. G. *MDR*, p. 379.

37. Jung, C. G. *MDR*, pp. 380–81.

38. Jung, C. G. *MDR*, p. 382.

39. Jung, C. G. *MDR*, pp. 382–83.

40. Jung, C. G. *MDR*, pp. 383–85.

41. Jung, C. G. *MDR*, p. 385.

42. Jung, C. G. *MDR*, pp. 386–88.

43. Jung, C. G. *MDR*, p. 388.

44. Jung, C. G. *MDR*, p. 389.

45. Lao Tzu. *TTC*, Mair, no. 4 (40), p. 8.

46. Lao Tzu. *TTC*, Mitchell, no. 2.

47. Lao Tzu. *TTC*, Mitchell, no. 6.

48. Lao Tzu. *TTC*, Mitchell, no. 16.

49. Lao Tzu. *TTC*, Mitchell, no. 21.

50. Lao Tzu. *TTC*, Mitchell, no. 22.

51. Lao Tzu. *TTC*, Mitchell, no. 28.

52. Lao Tzu. *TTC*, Wilhelm, no. 32, p. 41.

53. Lao Tzu. *TTC*, Wilhelm, no. 33, p. 41.

54. Lao Tzu. *TTC*, Wilhelm, no. 41, p. 46.

55. Lao Tzu. *TTC*, Wilhelm, no. 50, p. 49.

56. Lao Tzu. *TTC*, Wilhelm, no. 52, p. 50.

57. Lao Tzu. *TTC*, Wilhelm, no. 52, p. 50.

58. Chuang Tzu. *WCT*, p. 193.

59. Chuang Tzu. *WCT*, pp. 55–57.

60. Chuang Tzu. *WCT*, p. 61.

61. Chuang Tzu. *WCT*, p. 109.

62. Jung, C. G. *MDR*, p. 195.

63. Lao Tzu. *TTC*, Wilhelm, no. 25, p. 37.

64. Goethe, J. W. (1959) *Faust*, Part Two. Trans. P. Wayne. Harmondsworth, England: Penguin, p. 79.
"Recreation also has within it: re-creation! Play and rebirth!"

65. Jung, C. G. *MDR*, p. 196.

66. Jung, C. G. *MDR*, p. 196.

67. Jung, C. G. *MDR*, pp. 196–97.

68. Lao Tzu. *TTC*, Mitchell, no. 19.

69. Jung, C. G. (1921) *CW,* vol. 6, *Psychological Types.*

70. Jung, C. G. *CW*, vol. 6, *Psychological Types*, p. 217.

71. *The I. Ching*, Wilhelm and Baynes. Reference is to introduction by R. Wilhelm, p. LV.

72. Jung, C. G. *CW*, vol. 6, *Psychological Types*, p. 120.

73. Jung, C. G. *MDR*, pp. 207–8.

74. Jung, C. G. *MDR*, p. 223.

75. Baruch, F. "Jung and the Stone," *Mantis* 4, no. 1 (Winter 1991): 20–33. *Mantis* is the publication of the Cape of Good Hope Centre for Jungian Studies in Cape Town, South Africa.

76. Jung, C. G. *MDR*, pp. 223–24.

77. Jung, C. G. *MDR*, p. 224.

78. Lü Tzu. *SGF-W*, pp. 62–63.

79. Jung, C. G. *MDR*, p. 225.

80. Jung, C. G. *MDR*, p. 68.

81. Chuang Tzu. "The Tower of the Spirit," in "Readings from Chuang Tzu," *WCT*, pp. 198–200.

82. Jaffé, A. *From the Life and Work of C. G. Jung*, pp. 132, 133.

83. Lao Tzu. *TTC*, Mitchell, no. 42.
84. Lao Tzu. *Wen-tzu.* no. 42, pp. 43–44.
85. Lao Tzu. *TTC*, Mitchell, no. 6.

Chapter 5

1. Jung, C. G. "Commentary" to *SGF-W*, p. 85.
2. Jung, C. G. (1968) *CW*, vol. 13, *Alchemical Studies*, p. 18.
3. Jung, C. G. *MDR*, p. 247.
4. Jung, C. G. *MDR*, p. 248.
5. Jung, C. G. *MDR*, pp. 247–48.
6. Jung, C. G. *MDR*, p. 248.
7. Jung, C. G. *MDR*, p. 248.
8. Lao Tzu. *TTC*, Mitchell, no. 28.
9. Jung, C. G. *MDR*, p. 255.
10. Jung, C. G. *MDR*, p. 255.
11. Lao Tzu. *TTC*, Mitchell, no. 11.
12. Lao Tzu. *TTC*, Mitchell, no. 40.
13. Jung, C. G. *MDR*, p. 265.
14. Jung, C. G. *MDR*, p. 265.
15. Jung, C. G. *MDR*, p. 264.
16. Jung, C. G. (1954) "Marriage as a Psychological Relationship," in *CW* vol. 17, *The Development of Personality*, p. 168.
17. Jung, C. G. "Marriage as a Psychological Relationship," in *CW*, vol. 17, *The Development of Personality*, pp. 173, 176.
18. Lao Tzu. *TTC*, Wilhelm, no. 28, p. 39.
19. Lao Tzu. *TTC*, Mitchell, no. 42.
20. Cooper, J. C. (1990) *Chinese Alchemy: The Taoist Quest for Immortality.* New York: Sterling Publishing Co., p. 107.
21. Cooper, J. C. *Chinese Alchemy*, p. 107.
22. Cooper, J. C. *Chinese Alchemy*, p. 108.
23. Jung, C. G. "Commentary," in *SGF-W*, p. 104.
24. Jung, C. G. (1962) "In Memory of Richard Wilhelm" (IMRW), in *SGF-W*, p. 139.
25. Jung, C. G. IMRW, in *SGF-W*, p. 140.
26. Jung, C. G. IMRW, in *SGF-W*, p. 138.
27. Jung, C. G. IMRW, in *SGF-W*, p. 138.
28. Jung, C. G. IMRW, in *SGF-W*, p. 138.
29. Jung, C. G. IMRW, in *SGF-W*, p. 139.
30. Jung, C. G. IMRW, in *SGF-W*, p. 145.
31. Jung, C. G. IMRW, in *SGF-W*, p. 145.

32. Jung, C. G. IMRW, in *SGF-W*, p. 147.

33. Jung, C. G. IMRW, in *SGF-W*, p. 149.

34. Jung, C. G. IMRW, in *SGF-W*, p. 149.

35. Jung, C. G. *MDR*, p. 197.

36. Jung, C. G. *MDR*, p. 197.

37. Jung, C. G. *MDR*, p. 197.

38. Jung, C. G. *MDR*, p. 197.

39. Jung, C. G. *MDR*, p. 199.

40. Jung, C. G. "Commentary," in *SGF-W*, p. 86.

41. Jung, C. G. IMRW, in *SGF-W*, p. 144.

42. Jung, C. G. "Commentary," in *SGF-W*, p. 86.

43. Jung, C. G. (1928–31) Retitled "The Spiritual Problem of Modern Man," in *CW*, vol. 10, *Civilization in Transition*.

44. Jung, C. G. (1928–31) "The Spiritual Problem of Modern Man," *CW*, vol. 10, p. 77.

45. Lao Tzu. *TTC*, Mitchell, no. 5.

46. Lao Tzu. *TTC*, Mitchell, no. 53.

47. Lao Tzu. *TTC*, Mitchell, no. 13.

48. Lao Tzu. *TTC*, Wilhelm, no. 13, p. 31.

49. After reviewing an early draft of this part of the book, Robert Hinshaw suggested that neither Kirsch nor Neumann could have served as a *Rebbe* for Jung. Hinshaw maintained that they were his students, so it involved the issue of the father not listening to his sons. Ironically, it represented what had happened to Jung when Freud could not hear and accept what he was saying. However, to Jung's credit, he kept the relationships alive with these two analysts and worked through his conflicts and eventually ended up being very close to both of them.

    Also, after reviewing a draft of this section of the book, Rabbi Levi Meier shared this: "I believe that Jung can still have a posthumous relationship with a *Rebbe*, through a Rabbi studying his writings and applying them to Judaic thought. I feel that what I do is a form of that process." Most meaningfully, Rabbi David Freeman, who is a Jungian analyst, concurred with Rabbi Meier's sentiment.

50. Meier, L. (1991) *Jewish Values in Jungian Psychology*. Lanham and London: University Press of America, p. 152.

51. Neumann, M. (1991) "On the Relationship Between Erich Neumann and C. G. Jung and the Question of Anti-Semitism," in A. Maidenbaum, and S. A. Martin, eds., *Lingering Shadows: Jungians, Freudians and Anti-Semitism*. Boston and London: Shambhala, p. 274.

52. Altmann, A. (1991) "The Meaning and Soul of 'Hear, O Israel,' "

in L. Meier, *Jewish Values in Jungian Psychology*. Lanham and London: University Press of America, pp. 51–70.

53. Kirsch, J. (1991) "Carl Gustav Jung and the Jews: The Real Story," in A. Maidenbaum, and S. A. Martin, eds., *Lingering Shadows*, pp. 79–80.

54. Jung, C. G. (1968) *CW*, vol. 9I, *The Archetypes and the Collective Unconscious*, p. 349.

55. Jacoby, M. "Antisemitismus—ein ewiges Schattenthema" ("Antisemitism—A Constant Shadow Theme"), *Analytische Psychologie* 23 (1992): 24–40.

56. Chuang Tzu. *Inner Chapters*, p. 48.

57. Jaffé, A. *From the Life and Work of C. G. Jung*, p. 92.

58. Jaffé, A. *From the Life and Work of C. G. Jung*, p. 92.

59. I would also add that this was said out of ignorance or denial (or both), since the Jews have taken the same language and culture to the four corners of the globe.

60. Jung, C. G. (1934) "The State of Psychotherapy Today," in *CW*, vol. 10, *Civilization in Transition*, pp. 165–66.

61. Jung, C. G. "The State of Psychotherapy Today," in *CW*, vol. 10, *Civilization in Transition*, pp. 165–66.

62. Maidenbaum, A. (1991) "Lingering Shadows: A Personal Perspective," in A. Maidenbaum, and S. A. Martin, eds., *Lingering Shadows*, pp. 291–300.

63. Jung, C. G. "The State of Psychotherapy Today," in *CW*, vol. 10, *Civilization in Transition*, pp. 165–66.

64. Jaffé, A. *From the Life and Work of C. G. Jung*, p. 85.

65. Jung, C. G. *MDR*, p. 185.

66. Merton, T. (1968) *Zen and the Birds of Appetite (ZBA)*. New York: New Directions, p. 55.

67. Suzuki, D. T. *Mysticism: East and West*, p. 41.

68. Jung, C. G. *MDR*, p. 185.

69. Jung, C. G. *MDR*, p. 185.

70. Kirsch, J. (1991). "Carl Gustav Jung and the Jews: The Real Story," in A. Maidenbaum, and S. A. Martin, eds., *Lingering Shadows*, p. 76.

71. Neumann, M. "On the Relationship Between Erich Neumann and C. G. Jung and the Question of Anti-Semitism," in A. Maidenbaum, and S. A. Martin, eds., *Lingering Shadows*, p. 286.

72. Neumann, M. "On the Relationship Between Erich Neumann and C. G. Jung and the Question of Anti-Semitism," in A. Maidenbaum, and S. A. Martin, eds., *Lingering Shadows*, p. 286.

73. Jung, C. G. *MDR*, p. 235.

74. Jung, C. G. *MDR*, p. 235.

75. Jung, C. G. *MDR*, p. 235. Later, when the original gate was walled up, Jung put the same words above the entrance to the second tower.

76. Jung, C. G. "Psychological Commentary on 'The Tibetan Book of the Dead,' " in *CW*, vol. 11, *Psychology and Religion: West and East*, pp. 509–58.

77. Jung, C. G. "Psychological Commentary on 'The Tibetan Book of the Dead,' " *CW*, vol. 11, *Psychology and Religion: West and East*, p. 510.

78. Jung, C. G. "Psychological Commentary on 'The Tibetan Book of the Dead,' " *CW*, vol. 11, *Psychology and Religion: West and East*, pp. 514–15.

79. Jung, C. G. *MDR*, p. 224–25.

80. Jung, C. G. (1936/1954) "Concerning the Archetypes, with Special Reference to the Anima Concept," in *CW*, vol. 9I, *The Archetypes and the Collective Unconscious*, pp. 54–72.

81. Jung, C. G. *CW*, vol. 11, "Psychology and Religion," in *Psychology and Religion: West and East*, pp. 3–105.

82. Jung, C. G. (1916/1957) "The Transcendent Function," in *CW*, vol. 8, *The Structure and Dynamics of the Psyche*, pp. 67–91.

83. Jung, C. G. (1957) "The Undiscovered Self. (Present and Future)," in *CW*, vol. 10, *Civilization in Transition*, pp. 245–305.

84. Jung, C. G. "The Undiscovered Self. (Present and Future)," in *CW*, vol. 10, *Civilization in Transition*, pp. 302–5.

85. Jung, C. G. (1938/1954) "Psychological Aspects of the Mother Archetype," in *CW*, vol. 9I, *The Archetypes of the Collective Unconscious*, pp. 75–110.

86. Jung, C. G. (1940/1950) "Concerning Rebirth," in *CW*, vol. 9I, *The Archetypes of the Collective Unconscious*, pp. 111–47.

87. Jung, C. G. *MDR*, p. 275.

88. Jung, C. G. *MDR*, p. 275.

89. Jung, C. G. *MDR*, p. 275.

90. Jung, C. G. *MDR*, p. 276.

91. Jung, C. G. *MDR*, p. 276–77.

92. Jung, C. G. *MDR*, p. 277.

93. Jung, C. G. *MDR*, pp. 278–79.

94. Merton, T. (1968) "The Study of Zen," in *ZBA*, p. 2.

95. Merton, T. (1968) "A Christian Looks at Zen," in *ZBA*, p. 37.

96. Merton, T. "The Study of Zen," in *ZBA*, pp. 37, 50.

97. Merton, T. "The Study of Zen," in *ZBA*, pp. 10, 51.

98. Merton, T. (1968) "D. T. Suzuki, The Man and His Work," in *ZBA*, pp. 59–66.

99. Jung, C. G. (1939) "Foreword to Suzuki's 'Introduction to Zen Buddhism,' " in *CW*, vol. 11, *Psychology and Religion: West and East*, pp. 538–57.

100. Merton, T. "D. T. Suzuki, The Man and His Work," in *ZBA*, p. 59.

101. Merton, T. "D. T. Suzuki, The Man and His Work," in *ZBA*, pp. 60, 61.

102. Jung, C. G. "Foreword to Suzuki's 'Introduction to Zen Buddhism,' " in *CW*, vol. 11, *Psychology and Religion: West and East*, p. 538.

103. Jung, C. G. "Foreword to Suzuki's 'Introduction to Zen Buddhism,' " in *CW*, vol. 11, *Psychology and Religion: West and East*, p. 539.

104. Jung, C. G. "Foreword to Suzuki's 'Introduction to Zen Buddhism,' " in *CW*, vol. 11, *Psychology and Religion: West and East*, p. 538.

105. Lao Tzu. *TTC*, Wilhelm, no. 56, p. 52.

106. Jung, C. G. "Foreword to Suzuki's 'Introduction to Zen Buddhism,' " in *CW*, vol. 11, *Psychology and Religion: West and East*, p. 546.

107. Jung, C. G. "Foreword to Suzuki's 'Introduction to Zen Buddhism,' " in *CW*, vol. 11, *Psychology and Religion: West and East*, p. 553.

108. Jung, C. G. "Foreword to Suzuki's 'Introduction to Zen Buddhism,' " in *CW*, vol. 11, *Psychology and Religion: West and East*, p. 554.

109. Jung, C. G. "Foreword to Suzuki's 'Introduction to Zen Buddhism,' " in *CW*, vol. 11, *Psychology and Religion: West and East*, p. 555.

110. Jung, C. G. "Foreword to Suzuki's 'Introduction to Zen Buddhism,' " in *CW*, vol. 11, *Psychology and Religion: West and East*, p. 556.

111. Jung, C. G. "Foreword to Suzuki's 'Introduction to Zen Buddhism,' " in *CW*, vol. 11, *Psychology and Religion: West and East*, p. 557.

112. Miyuki, M. (1992) "Self-Realization in the Ten Oxherding Pictures," in D. J. Meckel and R. L. Moore, eds., *Self and Liberation: The Jung/Buddhism Dialogue*. New York: Paulist Press, pp. 181–205.

113. Merton, T. "Nishida: A Zen Philosopher," in *ZBA*, pp. 67–70.

114. The original use of the "self-Self axis," although modified here, is credited to Sally Parks (1980) and her use of this expression in her unpublished thesis, "The Puer Aeternus and the Narcissistic Personality—Kindred Spirits," The Inter-Regional Society of Jungian Analysts.

115. Jung, C. G. "On the Discourses of the Buddha," in *CW*, vol. 18, p. 699.

116. Lü Tzu. *SGF-W*, p. 29.

117. Lü Tzu. *SGF-W*, p. 42.

118. Jung, C. G. "Commentary," in Lü Tzu, *SGF-W*, p. 102.

119. Jung, C. G. "Commentary," in Lü Tzu, *SGF-W*, p. 113.

120. Jung, C. G. "Commentary," in Lü Tzu, *SGF-W*, p. 82.

121. Lü Tzu. *SGF-W*, pp. 50–51.

122. Lü Tzu. *SGF-W*, p. 22.

123. Jung, C. G. "Commentary," in Lü Tzu, *SGF-W*, pp. 92, 93.

124. Lü Tzu. *SGF-W*, p. 23.

125. I've expanded on the thesis of J. Sherry ("Jung, the Jews, and Hitler." *Spring,* 1986, vol. 46, pp. 163–75)—which purports that Jung's heart attack was precipitated by guilt he felt about the German psyche and his own—by suggesting that it encompass Jung's "soul/spirit attack" as well.

126. Jung, C. G. "After the Catastrophe," in *CW*, vol. 10, *Civilization in Transition*, pp. 194–95.

127. Jung, C. G. "After the Catastrophe," in *CW*, vol. 10, *Civilization in Transition*, pp. 194–95.

128. Jung, C. G. *MDR*, p. 294.

129. This is footnoted in *Memories, Dreams, Reflections: Pardes Rimmonim* is the title of an old Cabbalistic tract by Moses Cordovero (sixteenth century). In Cabbalistic doctrine Malchuth and Tifereth are two of the ten spheres of divine manifestation in which God emerges from his hidden state. They represent the female and male principles within the Godhead, p. 294.

130. Jung, C. G. *MDR*, p. 294.

131. Jung, C. G. *MDR*, p. 295.

132. Jung, C. G. *MDR*, p. 297.

133. Hannah, B. *J, H L & W*, p. 283.

134. Lü, Tung-pin. *SGF*. Trans. T. Cleary, p. 116.

135. Lü, Tung-pin. *SGF*, p. 113.

136. Lü, Tung-pin. *SGF*, p. 113.

137. As noted by B. Hannah, *J, H L & W*, p. 294.

138. Lao Tzu. *TTC*, Wilhelm, no. 10, p. 30.

Chapter 6

1. Lao Tzu. (1992) *Wen-tzu: Understanding the Mysteries*. Trans. T. Cleary. Boston and London: Shambhala, no. 54, p. 51.

2. Jung. C. G. *CW*, vol. 10, *Civilization in Transition*, p. 463.

3. *Webster's New World Dictionary of the American Language.* (1960) Cleveland and New York: The World Publishing Company, p. 1243.

4. Jung, C. G. *MDR*, p. 124.

5. van der Post, L. (1993) *The Voice of the Thunder*. London: Chatto & Windus, p. 174.

6. Hannah, B. *Jung, His Life and Work*, p. 186.

7. Hannah, B. *J, H L & W*, p. 185.

8. Jung, C. G. *MDR*, p. 198.

9. Jung, C. G. *MDR*, p. 198.

10. Hannah, B. *J, H L & W*, p. 186. After returning from Africa and before the dream, Hannah says Jung "suffered from a tendency to depression and a feeling of hopelessness."

11. Wilhelm, R. (1985) Introduction in Lao Tzu's *TTC*, Wilhelm, p. 13.

12. Jung, C. G. *MDR*, pp. 198–99.

13. Hannah, B. *J, H L & W*, p. 317.

14. Lao Tzu. *TTC*, Mair. No. 63 (in original, no. 19), p. 81.

15. Lao Tzu. *TTC*, Wilhelm, no. 28, p. 39.

16. Lao Tzu. *TTC*, Mitchell, no. 37.

17. Jung, C. G. *MDR*, p. 225.

18. Lao Tzu. *TTC*, Wilhelm, no. 1, p. 27.

19. Lao Tzu. *TTC*, Mitchell, no. 20.

20. Lao Tzu. *TTC*, Mitchell, no. 25.

21. Chuang Tzu. (1992) "Readings from Chuang Tzu," in *WCT*, p. 198.

22. Jung, *C. G. MDR*, pp. 225–26. During my visit to Bollingen, March 10, 1994, I learned (saw and experienced) how the Jung family has honored C. G. Jung's spirit. Bollingen was left to his heirs and they rotate spending time there. To the Jung family, the place remains as it was and there are still no modern conveniences: electricity, telephone, running water, toilet, etc.

23. Jung, C. G. *MDR*, p. 226. Noted in a footnote: "Title of an old Chinese woodcut showing a little old man in a heroic landscape." We will return to this very quote, after Jung's wife dies in 1955.

24. Jung, C. G. *MDR*, p. 226.

25. Chuang Tzu, "The Flight of Lin Hui," in "Readings from Chuang Tzu," *WCT*, p. 172.

26. Jung, C. G. *MDR*, p. 173.

27. Jung, C. G. *MDR*, p. 174.

28. Jung, C. G. *MDR*, p. 174.

29. Jung, C. G. *MDR*, p. 174.

30. Rosen, D. H. (1996) *Transforming Depression: Healing the Soul Through Creativity*. New York: Penguin/Arkana.

31. Jung, C. G. *MDR*, p. 175.

32. Peter Jung has cherished memories of being with and playing with his grandfather at Bollingen. Such activities included waterworks, meditation, sailing, and working (chopping wood, painting, sweeping,

etc.). Peter was twenty-one years old when C. G. Jung died in 1961, so he fondly remembers the golden period of Jung's life, especially the sunset years.

33. Jung, C. G. (1951) "On the Self" (incorporated as chapter 4), in *CW*, vol. 9II, *Aion*, pp. 23–35.

34. Jung, C. G. (1985) Foreword (1950) to *The I Ching*, 3d ed. Trans. R. Wilhelm (German) and C. F. Baynes (English). Princeton: Princeton University Press, p. xxiv.

35. Jung, C. G. *MDR*, p. 400.

36. *The I Ching*, Wilhelm, p. 642.

37. Jung, C. G. Foreword to *The I Ching*, p. xxvii.

38. Jung, C. G. Foreword to *The I Ching*, p. xxviii.

39. Jung, C. G. Foreword to *The I Ching*, p. xxvi.

40. Jung, C. G. Foreword to *The I Ching*, p. xxxi.

41. Jung, C. G. Foreword to *The I Ching*, p. xxxi.

42. Jung, C. G. Foreword to *The I Ching*, p. xxxii.

43. Jung, C. G. Foreword to *The I Ching*, pp. xxxiii–xxxv.

44. *The I Ching*, Wilhelm, p. 531.

45. Jung, C. G. Foreword to *The I Ching*, p. xxxvi.

46. *The I Ching*, Wilhelm, p. 629.

47. Jung, C. G. Foreword to *The I Ching*, p. xxxviii.

48. Jung, C. G. Foreword to *The I Ching*, p. xxxix.

49. Blofeld, T. (1991) *I Ching: The Book of Change*. New York: Penguin/Arkana.

50. Blofeld, T. *I Ching: The Book of Change*, p. 25.

51. Blofeld, T. *I Ching: The Book of Change*, p. 25.

52. Blofeld, T. *I Ching: The Book of Change*, p. 41.

53. Blofeld, T. *I Ching: The Book of Change*, p. 41.

54. Blofeld, T. *I Ching: The Book of Change*, p. 42.

55. Lao Tzu. (1990) *TTC*, Mair. This is an entirely new translation based on the recently discovered (1973) Ma-Wang-Tui manuscripts.

56. Lao Tzu. (1990) *Tao Te Ching*, Mair, no. 3 (no. 41 in standard translations), p. 7. Mair puts *Te* or Integrity first because that is how the order was in the Ma-Wang-Tui manuscripts.

57. Jung, C. G. *MDR*, p. 225.

58. Jung, C. G. *MDR*, p. 233.

59. Jung, C. G. *MDR*, pp. 235–36.

60. Jung, C. G. *MDR*, p. 237.

61. Jung, C. G. *MDR*, p. 237.

62. Lao Tzu. *TTC*, Mitchell, no. 14.

63. Jung, C. G. *MDR*, p. 297.

64. Lao Tzu. *TTC*, Wilhelm, no. 6, p. 29.

65. Lao Tzu. *TTC*, Mitchell. Notes on chapter 6, p. 88.

66. Jung, C. G. *MDR*, p. 20.

67. Jung, C. G. *MDR*, p. 42.

68. Jung, C. G. *MDR*, p. 42.

69. Jung, C. G. *MDR*, p. 42.

70. Jung, C. G. *MDR*, p. 68.

71. Jung, C. G. *MDR*, pp. 226–27. As noted in the footnote, the first sentence is a fragment from Heraclitus, the second sentence alludes to the Mithras liturgy, and the last sentence to Homer (*Odyssey*, book 24, verse 12).

72. Jung, C. G. *MDR*, pp. 227–28. Jung never carved the back face of the stone. As Jung stated: "Merlin . . . remains uncomprehended to this day!"

73. Lao Tzu. *TTC*, Mitchell, no. 27.

74. Jung, C. G. *Answer to Job*, in *CW*, vol. 11, *Psychology and Religion: West and East*.

75. Jung, C. G. (1952) "Synchronicity: An Acausal Connecting Principle," in *CW*, vol. 8, *The Structure and Dynamics of the Psyche*.

76. Lao Tzu. *TTC*. Mitchell, no. 5.

77. Jung, C. G., and W. Pauli. (1955) *The Interpretation of Nature and the Psyche*. New York: Pantheon.

78. Jung, C. G. *Letters*, vol. 2 (1975) Princeton, NJ: Princeton University Press, pp. 108–109.

79. Lao Tzu. *TTC*. Mitchell, no. 27.

80. Jung, C. G. "Synchronicity: An Acausal Connecting Principle," in *CW*, vol. 8, *The Structure and Dynamics of the Psyche*, pp. 515–17.

81. Gleick, J. (1988) *Chaos: Making a New Science*. New York: Penguin Books. Ironically, there is no mention of Jung's work in this otherwise excellent work.

82. Gleick, J. *Chaos: Making a New Science*, p. 43.

83. Hannah, B. *Jung, His Life and Work*, p. 308.

84. Hannah, B. *J, H L & W*, p. 313.

85. Hannah, B. *J, H L & W*, p. 313.

86. Jung, C. G. *CW*, vol. 14, pp. 463–64.

87. Chuang Tzu. "Readings from Chuang Tzu," *WCT*, p. 109.

88. Jung, C. G. "Commentary" on *SGF-W*, p. 102.

89. Jung, C. G. *MDR*, p. 225.

90. Lao Tzu. *TTC*, Mitchell, no. 39.

91. Lao Tzu. *TTC*, Mitchell, no. 59.

92. Hannah, B. *J, H L & W*, p. 326.

93. Hannah, B. *J, H L & W*, p. 329.

94. Jung, C. G. *MDR*, p. 175.

95. Jung, C. G. (1975) *C. G. Jung Letters*, vol. II: 1951–1961. Selected and edited by Gerhard Adler, in collaboration with Aniela Jaffé. Trans. R. F. C. Hull. Princeton: Princeton University Press, p. 293.

96. Jung, C. G. *MDR*, p. 134.

97. Jung, C. G. *MDR*, p. 256.

98. Jung, C. G. *CW*, vol. 15. *The Spirit in Man, Art, and Literature*, p. 59.

99. Jung, C. G. *MDR*, p. 325.

100. Jung, C. G. *MDR*, p. 326.

101. Hannah, B. *J, H L & W*, p. 344.

102. Jung, C. G. (1964) *Man and His Symbols* New York: Doubleday & Co.

103. Hannah, B. *J, H L & W*, p. 154.

104. Jung, C. G. *MDR*, pp. 358–59.

105. Von Franz, M. L. Personal communication, April 5, 1994.

106. Jung, C. G. *CW*, vol. 9I, *The Archetypes and the Collective Unconscious*, p. 37.

107. Jung, C. G. *MDR*, p. 359.

108. Chuang Tzu. *IC*, p. 30.

109. Jung, C. G. *CW*, vol. 10, *Civilization in Transition*, p. 407.

110. Jung, C. G. *CW*, vol. 10, p. 463.

111. Lao Tzu. *TTC*, Mitchell, no. 33.

112. Lao Tzu. *TTC*, Mitchell, no. 50.

113. Lao Tzu. *TTC*, Mitchell, no. 52.

114. Hannah, B. *J, H L & W*, p. 347.

115. Merton, T. *ZBA*, p. 8.

116. Merton, T. *ZBA*, p. 8.

117. Buber, M. (1990) *The Way of Man*. New York: Citadel/Carol, p. 13.

118. Buber, M. *The Way of Man*, p. 16.

119. Buber, M. *The Way of Man*, pp. 20, 25.

120. Buber, M. *The Way of Man*, p. 40.

121. Buber, M. *The Way of Man*, p. 41.

122. Lao Tzu. *TTC*, Mitchell, no. 54.

123. Lao Tzu. *TTC*, Mitchell, no. 67.

124. Lao Tzu. *TTC*, Mair, no. 17 (54), p. 23.

Epilogue

1. Jung, C. G. (1969) *The Archetypes and the Collective Unconscious*, CW, vol. 9I. Princeton: Princeton University Press, p. 290.

2. Lao Tzu. *Tao Te Ching*, chapter 21, trans. Carol Baumann, in "Time and Tao," *Spring*, 1951: 30.

3. "Naïve" means, at its root, "natural." It also suggests spontaneity unchecked by convention.

4. Guggenbühl-Craig, A. (1977) *Marriage: Dead or Alive*. Dallas: Spring Publications.

5. To be fair to my ex-wife, it is true that, at times, we both considered divorce, but I was reluctant to file because I'd been a child of divorce and I knew the pain our three children would face. I really felt we ought to find a way to endure (regardless of the pain and suffering) and to eventually forgive. In other words, I felt we needed to find a way to allow our marriage to individuate.

6. Rosen, D. H. (1996) *Transforming Depression: Healing the Soul Through Creativity* New York: Penguin/Arkana, pp. xvii–xxxii.

Suggested Readings

Beebe, J. (1992) *Integrity in Depth*. College Station, Texas: Texas A&M University Press; (1995, paperback ed.) New York: Fromm International.

Blofeld, J. (trans. and ed.) (1991) *I Ching: The Book of Change*. New York: Arkana/Penguin.

Campbell, J., ed. (1976) *The Portable Jung*. New York: Penguin.

Chuang Tzu. (1964) *The Complete Works of Chuang Tzu*. Trans. B. Watson. New York: Columbia University Press.

————. (1974) *Inner Chapters*. Trans. G-F. Feng and J. English. New York: Vintage Books.

————. (1992) "Readings from Chuang Tzu," in T. Merton's *The Way of Chuang tzu*. Boston: Shambhala.

Estés, C. P. (1992) *Women Who Run with the Wolves*. New York: Ballantine Books.

Hall, J. A. (1986) *The Jungian Experience: Analysis and Individuation*. Toronto: Inner City Books.

Hoff, B. (1983) *The Tao of Pooh*. New York: Penguin.

Jung, C. G. (1957–1979) *Collected Works*. 20 vols. Princeton: Princeton University Press.

————. (1963) *Memories, Dreams, Reflections*. Recorded and edited by Aniele Jaffé. New York: Pantheon.

———. *(1964)* *Man and His Symbols.* New York: Doubleday.

———. (1973, 1975) *Letters.* Vols. 1 and 2. Princeton: Princeton University Press.

Kast, Verena. (1986) *The Nature of Love.* Wilmette, Illinois: Chiron.

———. (1991) *Joy, Inspiration, and Hope.* College Station, Texas: Texas A&M University Press; (1994, paperback ed.) New York: Fromm International.

Kawai, H. (1996) *Buddhism and the Art of Psychotherapy.* College Station, TX: Texas A&M University Press.

Lao Tzu. (1972) *Tao Te Ching.* Trans. G-F. Feng and J. English. New York: Vintage Books.

———. (1985) *Tao Te Ching: The Richard Wilhelm Edition.* London and New York: Penguin/Arkana.

———. (1988) *Tao Te Ching.* Trans. S. Mitchell. New York: HarperCollins.

———. (1990) *Tao Te Ching: The Classic Book of Integrity and the Way.* Trans. V. A. Mair. New York: Bantam Books.

———. (1992) *Wen-tzu: Understanding the Mysteries.* Trans. T. Cleary. Boston: Shambhala.

Lü, Tung-pin. (1962) *The Secret of the Golden Flower: A Chinese Book of Life.* Trans. R. Wilhelm, with a commentary by C. G. Jung. New York: Harvest/Harcourt Brace Jovanovich.

McGuire, W., ed. (1974) *The Freud/Jung Letters.* Trans. R. Mannheim and R. F. C. Hull. Princeton: Princeton University Press.

Meckel, D.J. & Moore, R.L., (eds.) (1992) *Self and Liberation: The Jung–Buddhism Dialogue.* New York: Paulist Press.

Merton, T. (1975) *The Asian Journal.* New York: New Directions.

Moore, T. (1992) *Care of the Soul.* New York: HarperCollins.

Rosen, D. (1996) *Transforming Depression: Healing the Soul Through Creativity.* New York: Penguin/Arkana.

Samuels, A. (1985) *Jung and the Post-Jungians.* London and New York: Routledge.

Singer, J. (1994) *Boundaries of the Soul.* 2d ed. New York: Anchor/Doubleday.

Stein, M. (ed) 1984. *Jungian Analysis.* Boston: Shambhala.

Stevens, A. (1991) *On Jung.* New York: Penguin.

———. (1993) *The Million-Year-Old Self.* College Station, Texas: Texas A&M University Press; (1996, paperback ed.) New York: Fromm International.

Van der Post, L. (1977) *Jung and the Story of Our Time.* New York: Vintage Books.

Wehr, D. S. (1987) *Jung & Feminism: Liberating Archetypes.* Boston: Beacon Press.

Whitmont, E. C. & Perera, S. B. (1989) *Dreams, A Portal to the Source.* New York: Routledge.

Wilhelm, R. and C. Baynes, (trans.) (1967) *The I Ching or Book of Changes.* Princeton: Princeton University Press.

Woodman, M. (1982) *Addition to Perfection.* Toronto: Inner City Books.

Young-Eisendrath, Polly. (1993) *You're Not What I Expected: Learning to Love the Opposite Sex.* New York: William Morrow; (1994, paperback ed.) New York: Simon & Schuster/Touchstone.

———. (1996) *The Gifts of Suffering: Finding Insight, Compassion and Renewal.* New York: Addison-Wesley.

Index